BRIAN JOHNSTON'S
GUIDE TO CRICKET

BRIAN JOHNSTON'S GUIDE TO CRICKET

W.H. ALLEN · LONDON

Copyright © Brian Johnston, 1972, 1978, 1986

First published by W.H. Allen & Co. Ltd. in 1972 under the title
All About Cricket
Published by Carousel in 1974, reprinted 1975, 1978

Set in Plantin by
Phoenix Photosetting, Chatham
Printed and bound in Great Britain by
Mackays of Chatham Ltd, Kent
for the Publishers, W.H. Allen & Co. Plc
44 Hill Street, London W1X 8LB

British Library Cataloguing in Publication Data
Johnston, Brian
    Brian Johnston's guide to cricket. —
    Rev and updated ed.
    1. Cricket
    I. Title   II. Johnston, Brian
    All about cricket
    796.35'8   GV917

    ISBN 0-491-03922-0

Contents

	Acknowledgements	7
	Preface	9
1	The Story of Cricket	10
2	The Organization of Cricket	26
3	The Main Competitions	29
4	The Ashes	46
5	Test Matches – Six of the Best	51
6	My Forty-two Greats	80
7	The Main Techniques	148
8	Ten Ways of Getting Out	169
9	A Short Quiz	173
10	The Tale End	176
	Appendices	183
	Appendix 1: Glossary of Terms and Equipment	185
	Appendix 2: Main Cricket Records	209
	Appendix 3: Plans of the Six Test Match Grounds	221
	Appendix 4: Starting a Cricket Library	227
	Appendix 5: Answers to the Quiz	229
	Index	235

Acknowledgements

It would not be possible to write a book like this without the help and kindness of a great many people, and I would like to thank very sincerely all those who have helped me for their patience and understanding, especially the following:

Bill Frindall for his records and statistics which I could not possibly have done myself; Stephen Green, Curator of the MCC Museum; Donald Carr, Michael Gear and Brian Langley of the TCCB for their patience and good humour in answering so many of my questions.

Photographs in the book appear by kind permission of: Sport and General Press Agency Ltd; The Photo Source; BBC Hulton Picture Library.

Thanks are also due to the secretaries of the six cricket clubs who kindly provided plans of the six Test grounds.

Preface

In 1972 I was asked by W.H. Allen to write a book on cricket in their 'All About' series. My first reaction was to think how presumptuous it would be for me to write '*All* About Cricket'. It was such a vast subject and who was I to undertake such a task? But I then thought of all the joy and pleasure which I myself had got out of cricket. Since I was seven years old it had been a large part of my life. If only I could bring the game into other people's lives – especially for the young for whom the series was really intended. It was vital to sell the game to young people in an era where there is so much competition from other sports and activities. So I wrote the book as a useful guide as to what cricket *is* all about, and to try to encourage young readers to play, watch or read about the game. I felt that if they could, as a result, also *live* cricket as I have done, it was something they would never regret.

Now fourteen years later I have been asked to bring 'All About Cricket' up to date under a less arrogant title! After forty years of commentating I still feel the urge to 'sell' cricket. So here is a mixture of the history of the game, its organization, competitions and laws. There's a glossary of cricketing terms and a coaching guide on techniques. For good measure I have included a quiz, a few of the best cricket stories, and advice on how to start a library. I hope it will bring cricket into *your* life.

Brian Johnston
St John's Wood
January 1986

The Story of Cricket

THE STORY OF cricket is not easy to write. There is no definite beginning and so far, thank goodness, no end. Nobody knows when it started and, in spite of some critics who have forecast its demise for the last ninety years or more, it is still very much alive. One can only imagine that many hundreds of years ago some boy started throwing stones at a friend who, to protect himself, picked up a stick and tried to hit them back. The derivation of the word cricket could easily come from the shepherd's crook which would have made the best available bat and could account for the curved shape of the early bats. They were not unlike a hockey stick – a shape very suitable for dealing with the bowling of those days which was usually along the ground. Similarly the wicket which was originally two stumps with one bail, could have started life as the small wicket gate through which sheep entered a field or pen.

As far back as 1272 there is mention of King Edward the First's son, Prince Edward, playing *Creag*, and this is surely sufficient proof that cricket was already a game by then. But the first definite proof seems to be a manuscript dated 16 January 1598, which is now in the possession of the Mayor of Guildford. It refers to a Surrey coroner, John Derwick, 'playing at crickett' when he was 'a scholler of the free school of Guildford'. From then on there are various references in 1622, 1647, and 1654 to people being fined for playing cricket on Sundays. It had even spread overseas as Cromwell's generals are said to have 'prohibited crickett' in Ireland. It seems likely that, with Cromwell in power in England, the game caught on with the nobility who, with no court in London, retired to their country estates. They found that cricket was not only fun to play but that it also provided them with an opportunity to gamble. Whether we like it or not much of the cricket played from then on was the occasion for betting on the results of matches.

All evidence shows that the early development of cricket centred on the counties of Hampshire, Kent, Surrey, and Sussex, and also on London itself. In fact, the first surviving score sheet is of Kent *v.* England at the Artillery Grounds in the City of London on 18 June

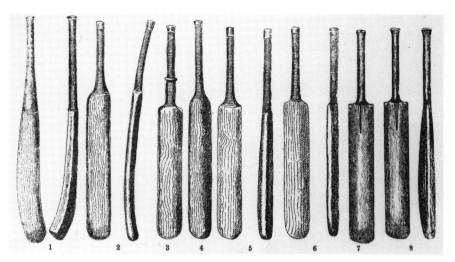

A collection of eighteenth and nineteenth
century bats. No. 1, 1743; No. 2, 1771;
No. 3, 1790; No. 4, 1792; No. 5, 1800;
No. 6, 1827; Nos. 7 and 8
illustrate the art of splicing.

1746 – Kent winning a four-innings match by 1 wicket, and 18 being
the highest individual score. There are various accounts of other
matches during this period, at Penshurst, Kensington Gardens,
Mitcham, and above all at Hambledon, a small village just north of
Portsmouth. A short account of this famous club will help more
than anything else to show what cricket in the eighteenth century
was like and how its laws gradually developed.

The club was formed some time around 1750 and its first Captain
and Secretary was Richard Nyren, landlord of the Bat and Ball Inn,
which was situated alongside Broad Halfpenny Down, the ground
on which they played. This small village attracted players from the
surrounding districts and became strong enough to take on and beat
the full strength of England. They took part in the first recorded tie
– against Kent in 1783. 'Old' John Small, their best batsman and a
bit of a dab on the fiddle when the game was over, made the first
recorded century – 136 *v*. Surrey. Richard Nyren's son, John, in his
Young Cricketer's Tutor has brought to life many of their players –
Thomas Brett, who bowled fast and straight lobs (there was no
over-arm or round-arm bowling yet), and Tom Sueter who kept
wicket to him with no gloves or pads, supported by George Leer 'as
sure as a sandbank' at long-stop. Both Sueter and Leer had fine
tenor voices and led the singing in the Bat and Ball. Then there was
the left-handed gipsy, Noah Mann, a fine all-rounder and horseman

The Bat and Ball Inn, Hambledon, in 1908.

who rode twenty miles to play. Their greatest bowler and the most accurate of his time was David Harris, and, as Hambledon's fortunes began to decline, 'Silver Billy' Beldham appeared, a prolific run-getter who came from Farnham in Surrey but played for Hambledon.

Towards the end of the century London became more and more the centre of cricket. Betting on the game was increasing and as early as 1774 it became necessary to standardize various weights and measurements, some of which are still the same today (e.g. the weight of the ball between 5½ and 5¾ ozs, and the width of the bat 4¼ inches). There was also the first mention of an lbw law at this time. Thus the game gradually developed and in 1775 Hambledon played Kent in a five-a-side match at the Artillery ground. When John Small went in to bat, 14 runs were needed. He got the runs all right but in the process several balls from 'Lumpy' Stevens passed between the two stumps. Accordingly a third stump was added, although the size of the wicket remained the same. About ten years later a second bail was also added and the wicket began to look like the one we know today.

At this time the White Conduit Club was flourishing at Islington but its members wanted to find another ground as new buildings were ruining their privacy. They therefore asked a Yorkshireman living in London called Thomas Lord to find them a new ground.

He agreed and chose a piece of land in Marylebone where Dorset Square now stands. He took out a twenty-one-year lease and the first match was played there in 1787, and in that year the members of the White Conduit Club formed the Marylebone Cricket Club – the MCC. A year later MCC revised the laws as they then stood ('hit wicket' became a way of dismissal, and a batsman could only be out lbw if the ball pitched between wicket and wicket). From that day MCC became the unofficial rulers of the game – responsible for its administration and laws.

When Thomas Lord's lease ran out in 1808 he negotiated for a new piece of land at North Bank, Regent's Park. This was only used for three seasons and then building and railway development forced Lord to move once again. So still with his original turf from Dorset Square he moved to the present site of Lord's in St John's Wood, where the first match was played on 22 June 1814. Since then, Lord's has been the acknowledged headquarters of cricket. From then on the development of cricket to the game we know now received a new impetus, and it spread rapidly throughout the

The famous sign of the Bat and Ball Inn.

Kent *v.* Sussex at Brighton, 1849.

country. There were a lot of 'firsts' round about this time too. The first Gentlemen *v.* Players was played in 1806, the first recorded double century was 278 by William Ward for MCC *v.* Norfolk at Lord's in 1820, and the first University match took place in 1827. Incidentally, playing for Norfolk in that 1820 match was a seventeen-year-old batsman – Fuller Pilch, who later played for Kent and was one of the greatest batsmen ever. By 1835 round-arm bowling was finally legalized in a thorough revision of the laws by MCC which included standardizing the length of the bat to its present 38 inches and the introduction of the 'follow on' rule.

At about this time also County cricket began to get on to an organized footing and county clubs were formed – Sussex being the first in 1839.

Famous names appear in the score sheets – John Wisden, who later published the first *Wisden Almanack* in 1864, and who bowled ten batsmen in one innings for North *v.* South, and George Parr after whom Parr's tree at Trent Bridge was named; Alfred Mynn the 'Lion of Kent', over 6 feet tall and weighing 20 stone, and Felix, also of Kent, who was as stylish a batsman as he was an artist. With the opening of Trent Bridge by William Clark in 1838 cricket for the first time had become popular in the north, and Clark organized an

'How's that?' From a drawing by N. Felix, 1853.

England's first-ever touring team.

All-England XI which travelled round the country playing every type of club, large and small.

Then in 1859 came a milestone when a team of English cricketers captained by George Parr set sail for Canada to become the first-ever cricket touring team. Nine years later a team of Australian Aborigines visited England. These events provide us with a good opportunity to check on how cricket had spread overseas. The starting dates are all rather vague, but it is clear that in most cases it was the British Army or Navy who introduced cricket to the colonies.

In Australia a British colony was established at Botany Bay in 1788 and no doubt they played cricket. But it is not until 1830 that we find the first account of a game played in Sydney and the formation of the first club in Hobart, Tasmania, two years later. In 1845 the Melbourne CC was formed and with the same initials as our own MCC similarly became the centre of administration. The game soon spread to all the other states and it took such a hold that the catering firm of Spiers and Pond sponsored the first-ever teams from England to visit Australia in 1861 and 1863. Both incidentally made a good profit. In 1876 another team came from England, captained by J Lillywhite, and in March 1877 they played the first-ever Test at Melbourne, which Australia won by 45 runs. Finally, the Australian cricket scene was complete when the Earl of Sheffield donated 150 guineas for the promotion of cricket among the states and the Sheffield Shield competition came into being. At first only New South Wales, South Australia, and Victoria competed, but Queensland joined in 1926 and Western Australia in 1947, winning the Shield at their first attempt.

Cricket in South Africa was undoubtedly introduced by the British Army, which occupied the Cape at the end of the eighteenth century and the Cape Colony was the first centre of cricket in South Africa. But, as in Australia, it soon spread – Natal, Orange Free State, and Transvaal all forming clubs in quick succession. The first English team under C A Smith toured South Africa in 1888–89, winning both their Test matches, and, in the same season, Sir Donald Currie presented the Currie Cup for competition between the leading provinces.

Because of the amount of sea travel involved, cricket in the West Indies developed far more slowly. It seems to have started in Trinidad, Barbados, Jamaica, and British Guiana (now Guyana) in the early eighteenth century. However, it was not until 1894 that a team from England visited the islands, and the first official MCC tour did not take place until 1911. Similarly, regular organized competition between the islands was difficult to arrange. It is only during the last twenty years or so that air travel has made visits between the islands practical, resulting in the formation of the Shell Shield Tournament in 1965–66.

Cricket in New Zealand did not really begin until the second half of the nineteenth century, the first inter-provincial match taking place on North Island in March 1860 when Auckland played Wellington. Four years later the first first-class match was played on South Island, Otago beating Canterbury at Dunedin. A team from England under the captaincy of George Parr also played four matches in that year, while James Lillywhite's team visited New Zealand after their Australian tour of 1877. One year later the first Australian team came over on their way to England. But it is remarkable that these two near neighbours – in spite of occasional unofficial visits – have only played twenty-one official Test matches. New Zealand's inter-provincial competition is the Plunket Shield, presented by Lord Plunket when Governor-General in 1906, the first match being played in 1907.

Although India came late on to the Test scene, thanks to the British Army, cricket dates back to well before the start of the nineteenth century, although first-class cricket was not played until 1892. The first English team went out under G F Vernon in 1889, but the first MCC team to play Tests in India was that captained by D R Jardine in 1933–34. Until the start of the Ranji Trophy Competition in the same year, first-class cricket had been rarely played but since then it has flourished.

Pakistan, of course, only became a separate cricketing country after partition in 1947. But in 1952 they were playing their first Test against India, and by 1957 had already chalked up victories against both England and Australia.

Sri Lanka played their first Test in 1982.

The countries I have mentioned are the 'senior' members of the International Cricket Conference and as such are the only countries to play Test matches. But cricket has been played wherever British influence has existed and that, at one time or another, has meant virtually the whole world. In Europe, Holland and Denmark are the main contenders and many club tours are arranged between them and England. Portugal, Germany, and Italy have all been cricket strongholds from time to time and, believe it or not, cricket is played in Paris, North, Central, and South America, Canada, Fiji, Hong Kong, Egypt, Corfu, Kenya, Nigeria, Burma, and Malaysia. The list is never-ending – even Turkey and Greece have been known to stage a game. Such is the appeal of cricket – loved by many and yet completely incomprehensible to many others. But whenever two or three of British stock are gathered together you can be sure that cricket will be played so long as they can 'bully' enough of the 'natives' to join them!

The return from Australia in 1864 of the second English touring team heralded one of the most important years in English cricket. Over-arm bowling was at last legalized. Surrey became the first-ever County Champions and the first issue of *Wisden's Cricketers' Almanack* was published. Even more important, two days before his sixteenth birthday, W G Grace made his first appearance in big cricket, scoring 170 and 56 not out for South Wales Club *v.* Gentlemen of Sussex. From then on this bearded giant of a man strode supreme across the English cricket scene until just after the turn of the century. He actually played his last game of cricket in July 1914, a few days after his sixty-sixth birthday. During that time he *was* Cricket to the whole of England. People travelled miles in their gigs or pony carts to catch a sight of him playing. For over thirty-five years he hit the headlines. He was to cricket then, what until recently Lester Piggott was to racing, or Pele was to soccer. He created many records in first-class cricket. He was the first to make

The great Dr W. G. Grace.

2,000 runs in a season; to do the double of 1,000 runs and 100 wickets; to score 200 and 300 runs in an innings; to reach 100 centuries; to make 1,000 runs in May. It is impossible to compare fairly cricketers of one generation with another. But remembering the bad pitches on which he had to make most of his runs, there has surely never been a greater cricketer, nor a more powerful personality. Cricket built on the foundations of his success, and from the day he appeared on the scene developments came thick and fast.

In 1868 the first touring team to visit England was a team of Aborigines from Australia and in 1876–77 Lillywhite's team toured Australia and played the first-ever Test match at Melbourne in March 1877. This was quickly followed by the first Australian team to tour England under the captaincy of D W Gregory, and they caused a sensation by beating MCC in a single day by 9 wickets. 1880 saw the first Test match in England when England beat W L Murdoch's side by 5 wickets. Two years later Australia had their revenge at the Oval by winning by 7 runs in the famous match which created the Ashes (see page 46).

So Test cricket was well and truly launched and MCC ensured the universal development of cricket by a complete revision of the Laws of Cricket in 1884. Except for occasional amendments they were not again fully revised until 1947. South Africa, New Zealand, England, and Australia – in that order – all set up their own Boards of Control and in 1909 the Imperial Cricket Conference was constituted, with England, Australia, and South Africa the original members. The County Championship, which had started in 1864, took time to catch on and by 1890 there were still only eight counties competing: Sussex, Nottinghamshire, Surrey, Kent, Yorkshire, Middlesex, Lancashire, and Gloucestershire. But by 1899 all but two of the present seventeen were included; Northamptonshire joining in 1905 and Glamorgan in 1921. Two years later the Minor County Championship was reorganized on its present basis.

All this time, of course, there were many great cricketers playing first-class cricket and I am conscious of the fact that I have so far only mentioned one, W G Grace. But it is difficult to strike the right balance between giving a catalogue of names and the danger of mentioning too few. However, from Australia there were W L Murdoch, Australia's first captain over here; C Bannerman, who scored the first-ever Test hundred (165 n.o.) in his first Test innings; F R Spofforth, 'the Demon' who took the first Test 'hat-trick'; G J Bonnor, the big hitter; G Giffen and C T B Turner, two great bowlers and J M Blackham, a magnificent wicket-keeper.

For England there was Arthur Shrewsbury, about whom W G said, 'Give me Arthur', when asked which batsman he rated the highest; A E Stoddart, a 'Rugger' International and fine athlete who captained England to victory in the 1894–95 series; R Peel, possibly the greatest of all the Yorkshire slow left-arm bowlers; A C Maclaren, whose 424 is still the highest individual score ever made in first-class cricket in England; K S Ranjitsinhji – 'Ranji' – one of cricket's greatest stroke players; the Hon. F S Jackson – 'Jacker' – who never toured overseas, but who was a super Test batsman, a good bowler, and not only won the toss five times in the 1905 series but also topped the batting and bowling averages and won the rubber; G A Lohmann, a match-winning, medium-pace bowler; and T Richardson and W H Lockwood, a great fast-bowling partnership.

Just before the end of the century the Board of Control was set up by the counties to run Test cricket in England and in 1899, for the first time, there was a Test series of five matches in England. In the same year a record was made which still stands today – the highest individual score in any class of cricket. This was 628 not out by A E J Collins for Clark's *v*. North Town, a junior house match at Clifton College. Even if he made 0 in all his other innings he must still have had a very good batting average at the end of the season!

For the next fourteen years cricket in England reached perhaps its highest peak. I myself would call it the 'Golden Age', though some writers give this accolade to the last decade of the nineteenth century. But just look at the names of some of those who played in this period, to which should be added most of those already mentioned. For England: C B Fry, G Gunn, P F Warner, J T Tyldesley, G H Hirst, G L Jessop, W Rhodes, J B Hobbs, F E Woolley, S F Barnes, R E Foster. For Australia: M A Noble, C Hill, V T Trumper, W W Armstrong, W Bardsley, J Darling, S E Gregory, C G Macartney. For South Africa: G A Faulkner, H W Taylor, P W Sherwell, R O Schwarz, A D Nourse, Senior. These are only a few of the great players of that time during which the first MCC team went to Australia (1903), South Africa played their first Test in England (1907), the Imperial Cricket Conference was constituted (1909), and the first and only Triangular Tournament was played between England, Australia, and South Africa (1912).

The period between the two wars saw the entry of the West Indies (1928), New Zealand (1930), and India (1932) into Test cricket. But inevitably the main 'enemy' was Australia, who swamped England for eight years after the war, thanks to some superb fast bowling by J M Gregory and E A McDonald, backed up by the spin of A A Mailey, and great batting strength made up largely from the pre-war batsmen. In reply England had to offer J B Hobbs and H Sutcliffe as the most successful-ever Test opening batting partnership, and M W Tate and H Larwood as top-quality medium and fast bowlers respectively. Larwood was to be at the centre of cricket's greatest storm – the body-line series between England and Australia in 1932–33 – a tour which nearly brought cricket relations between the

Sir John (Jack) Hobbs – the Master.

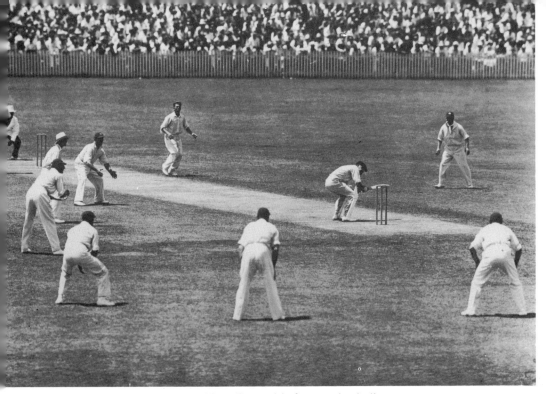
Harold Larwood bowling to his famous body-line
field in Brisbane, 1933.

two countries to an end. But looking back over the twenty-year
period, we see that three batsmen stand out above everything and
everybody else (even that superb spin-bowling partnership of
O'Reilly and Grimmett): J B Hobbs – the 'Master' the greatest
batsman ever on all types of pitches who made more hundreds (197)
and more runs (61,237) than any other player to date. D G Bradman
– the 'Don' – cricket's greatest run-making machine who in far
fewer innings than Hobbs (388 compared to 1,315) scored 28,067
runs (an average of 95.14 against Hobbs' 50.65), made 117 hundreds and in fifty-two Tests averaged 99.94! And thirdly, not far
behind, W R Hammond, a more brilliant bat than either and a fine
medium-pace bowler.

Before the start of the Second World War, England had regained
the Ashes in 1926, lost them in 1930, regained them in 1933, and lost
them again in 1934. South Africa had won their first Test in England
(1935). The West Indies, New Zealand, and India were elected
members of the Imperial Cricket Conference (1926) and four-day
Test matches were played for the first time in England in 1930.

When first-class cricket restarted after the war in 1946, the same
pattern emerged as in 1919. For seven years Australia was on top
and then, as before, the position was reversed with England holding

the Ashes for six years. After that they changed hands regularly (see page 48). All the other countries except for Sri Lanka were to defeat England in this country for the first time: The West Indies in 1950; Pakistan on their first tour in 1954; India in 1971 and New Zealand in 1983. In 1946 cricket lovers had been starved of cricket for six years and the crowds flocked to the ground to see personalities like Hutton, Bedser, Compton and Evans. 1947 will always be remembered as the 'Golden Year' when both Compton and Edrich made over 3,000 runs, Compton making 3,816 runs and scoring 18 hundreds, two records which still stand. Hobbs had been the Master, Bradman the run-machine and now Compton was the entertainer.

Both Bedser and Evans, too, can claim to have been the best in their own field: Bedser being the first England bowler to take 200 Test wickets, and Evans the first wicket-keeper to have over 200 Test victims. And last but not least, Hutton – the first professional ever appointed to captain England regularly. He captained the team which regained the Ashes in 1953, and his batting for its pure technique on all types of pitches, came nearest to that of Hobbs.

Since then many outstanding cricketers have played for England – May, Cowdrey, Dexter, Laker, Trueman, Boycott, Willis and Botham to name but a few. From overseas the most exceptional was Sobers, who, for those who never saw W G Grace, must qualify as the greatest all-rounder the world has ever seen. From Australia Harvey arguably the best of their left-handers, Greg Chappell top run getter, Lillee top wicket-taker. From West Indies the three 'W's' – Worrell, Weekes and Walcott, Lloyd, Richards, Gibbs and Holding. Graeme Pollock and Barry Richards from South Africa. Sutcliffe and Richard Hadlee from New Zealand. Gavaskar and Kapil Dev from India, Hanif Mohammad and Imran Khan from Pakistan. One could go on and on. The forty years since World War Two have certainly been rich in talent.

In those same forty years there have been more changes in the organization and laws of the game than at any time in its history. In 1947 there was a major revision of the laws – the first since 1884. A year later the first five-day Tests were played in England. In 1963 the amateur was abolished in English first-class cricket, and in 1965 the Imperial Cricket Conference became the International Cricket Conference. In 1980 there was another new code of laws.

But by far the most important change was the introduction of limited over cricket. The Gillette Cup was started in 1963, the John Player League in 1969 and the Benson and Hedges Cup in 1972. All three have been great successes and have attracted to the grounds many extra thousands for whom, in this space age, three-day cricket has become too slow. The modern spectator wants to see a result in one day. The exception to all this is Test cricket which although it lasts for five days, seems to be more popular than ever.

The popularity of the three one-day competitions has done much to help the financial position of the counties, many of whom were in dire straits. But this is nothing new. Cricket has usually been broke. In the old days it depended on the generosity of rich patrons; now it has to rely on similar generosity from sponsors. Sponsorship has spread to all classes of cricket – the three Prudential World Cups, the Texaco Trophy, the Cornhill Tests, the Britannic Assurance Championship, the William Younger Cup for Club Cricket, the Haig, Whitbread and now Norsk Hydro Fertilisers Cup for village cricket, and the Cricketer Cup for the old public school boys.

All this money is needed to pay for the ever increasing costs of running cricket. The game is as popular as ever. County Member-ships are up, more people are playing cricket, reading about it, watching on TV or listening to Test Match Special on the radio. The one worry is that in the schools there is not so much cricket played. The large comprehensives, the crowded schedules, the cost of maintaining cricket grounds, the lack of masters who can coach, the competition of non-team games – all these are reasons for it. On the other hand counties are doing far more to coach, and arrange games for schoolboys during their holidays.

For well over ninety years the approaching death of cricket has been regularly announced. In 1986 I am happy to announce that to me at least: 'Cricket is very much alive.'

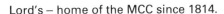

Lord's – home of the MCC since 1814.

The Organization of Cricket

THERE ARE MANY different forms of cricket played in Great Britain – Test matches, first-class cricket, Minor Counties, Knockout, and League competitions played by first-class cricketers, League, Club, Village, Women's, University, and School cricket. They all come under the first-ever *official* governing body for cricket – The Cricket Council. Before the Council's creation in 1969, MCC – a private member's club – had, by worldwide consent and goodwill, been accepted as *unofficially* responsible for the legislation of cricket.

MCC was formed in 1787 by members of the White Conduit Club, for whom Thomas Lord had opened his first ground in Dorset Fields, St Marylebone. MCC stands for Marylebone Cricket Club. The members inherited from White Conduit the task of framing the laws. Then at the beginning of this century the counties asked MCC to set up:

1. The Advisory County Cricket Committee to run the County Championship, (now the Britannic Assurance County Championship).

2. The Board of Control to organize Test matches in England. MCC itself was asked to organize all overseas tours.

In 1966 the Sports Council was set up by the Government with power to grant financial aid to all sports. They therefore asked MCC to set up an official body to run cricket, as they would not be able to deal with a private club. This led to the formation of the Cricket Council, which is twenty strong and has two executive wings. Its structure in 1985 was as follows:

Chairman

Vice-Chairman

Secretary

1. Test & County Cricket Board (8 representatives)

2. MCC (3 representatives)

3. National Cricket Association (5 representatives)

4. Minor Counties (1 representative)

5. Irish Cricket Union (1 representative)

6. Scottish Cricket Union (1 representative)

1. TEST AND COUNTY CRICKET BOARD
Now does the job of the Advisory County Cricket Committee and the Board of Control. It is responsible for:

a) All Test matches and first-class cricket in this country.

b) All overseas tours; the team is now no longer called MCC but England.

c) All knock-out and league competitions played by first- or second-class cricketers.

d) Minor Counties Cricket.

For voting purposes it consists of one member from each of the first-class counties, one from MCC and one from Minor Counties. The last two usually send two representatives and the universities, Irish and Scottish Union one each. But they *don't* have a vote.

2. MCC
Provides Lord's as the headquarters of cricket. The TCCB and NCA now have their own staff and no longer have their offices *in* the Lord's pavilion. They are now in a new building behind the tennis court and museum.

MCC is still responsible for the laws of cricket and for any changes made in them, but only after full consultation and agreement with all the overseas cricketing countries. But a new law can still only be made, or an old law changed, by the vote of MCC members at a general meeting of the club.

3. NATIONAL CRICKET ASSOCIATION
Is responsible for all other grades of cricket not covered by the Test and County Cricket Board. It is composed of representatives of schools, clubs, the Combined Services, Women's Cricket, the Universities, the Headmasters Conference and Umpires. It can also co-opt representatives from the National Playing Fields Association and the Central Council of Physical Recreation.

4. MINOR COUNTIES
The Minor Counties, first formed in 1895, consist of nineteen teams not considered good enough to be first class.

5. IRISH CRICKET UNION
Came into being in 1923.

6. SCOTTISH CRICKET UNION
Founded in 1909, though the Scottish XI had been playing representative matches since 1865.

In addition, there is the International Cricket Conference. Until 1965 this was called the Imperial Cricket Conference which had been founded in 1909 by England, Australia and South Africa. When South Africa withdrew from the Commonwealth in 1961, they automatically ceased to be members of the Imperial Cricket Conference.

When the Conference was renamed in 1965 membership was as follows:

a) *Full* membership is confined to the governing bodies of cricket in countries within the British Commonwealth where Test cricket is played i.e. England, Australia, India, New Zealand and West Indies (elected in 1926), Pakistan (elected in 1953) and Sri Lanka (elected in 1981).

b) From 1965 there have been associate members elected as follows:

i)   Fiji and USA in 1965.
ii)   Bermuda, Holland, Denmark, and East Africa in 1966.
iii)   Malaysia in 1967.
iv)   Canada in 1968.
v)   Gibraltar and Hong Kong in 1969.
vi)   Papua New Guinea in 1973.
vii)   Argentina, Israel, Singapore in 1974.
viii) West Africa in 1976.
ix)   Bangladesh in 1977.
x)   Kenya, Zimbabwe in 1981.

N.B. – The Chairman of the International Cricket Conference is automatically the president of MCC who also supply their secretary as secretary to the Conference.

The Main Competitions

IN ADDITION TO the hundreds of club, village, university, school and women's matches played all over Great Britain the main competitions are:

1. The Cornhill Test Matches.

2. The Britannic Assurance County Championship.

3. The NatWest Trophy.

4. The Benson and Hedges Cup.

5. The John Player Special League.

6. United Friendly Insurance Minor County Championship.

7. The Leagues in the North, Midlands, Scotland and Wales.

8. The William Younger Club Cup.

9. The Cricketer Cup for Old Public School Teams.

10. The Norsk Hydro Fertilisers National Village Championship.

11. International matches including the World Cup.

1. TEST MATCHES

In this country the Tests against the other six full members of the International Cricket Conference last for five days and are sponsored by Cornhill Insurance. The various series consist of 3 Tests, 5 Tests or 6 Tests; in England a 3 Test series is held when there is a double tour with two countries visiting, one in the first half of the summer, the other in the second half. The present regulation for the number of overs to be bowled in a day is 90.

Hours of Play
11 a.m. – 6.00 p.m. all five days or after 90 overs have been bowled (whichever is the later).
N.B. 1. If play is suspended (other than for normal intervals) the minimum number of overs to be bowled in the day shall be

reduced by one over for every full four minutes playing time lost.

2. In the event of play being suspended for one hour or more in aggregate on any of the *first four* days for any reason other than normal intervals, close of play on that day will be at 7.00 p.m. If the required minimum numbers of overs to be bowled have not been completed by 7.00 p.m., then play will continue until such time as they have been bowled.

Luncheon Interval
The luncheon interval is generally from 1.00 p.m. to 1.40 p.m. These timings may be varied if, owing to the weather or the state of the ground, an alteration has been agreed to by the captains or ordered by the umpires. For instance, lunch may be taken early in the hope that rain will stop. Or if an innings ends or there is a stoppage caused by weather or bad light within 10 minutes of the agreed time, the lunch interval will be taken immediately. But the interval is still restricted to 40 minutes and resumption of play would therefore be 40 minutes after the players had left the field.

Tea Interval
This takes place between 3.40 p.m. and 4.00 p.m. but may be taken early if there is an interruption for weather or bad light. If, on any of the first four days, play has been suspended for one hour or more prior to 3.40 p.m. and the time of close of play has been extended to 7.00 p.m., tea will be from 4.10 to 4.30 p.m.

Covering of pitches
The whole pitch *must* be covered:
a) The night before the match, and, if necessary, before the first ball is bowled. It must also be covered if necessary at any time before that during the preparation of the pitch.
b) On each night of the match, and if necessary, through Sunday.
c) In the event of play being suspended because of bad light or rain during the hours of play.

Fitness of pitch, ground, weather, light
All decisions concerning the fitness of the pitch, ground, weather or light for play will be *solely in the hands of the umpires*. Before suspending play for bad light they must ask the batting side whether they wish to continue. If they do, then play goes on. If, however, later the light deteriorates still further the batsmen may then appeal

to the umpires, who if they think that the light has got worse or the conditions are more dangerous since the batsmen decided to continue, may then suspend play.

2. THE BRITANNIC ASSURANCE COUNTY CHAMPIONSHIP

The first sponsorship of this was by Schweppes (from 1977 to 1983). Seventeen counties compete, each playing 24 matches. Illogically this means that although all counties meet each other at least once, they only play a return match against eight of the others. If at the end of the season two or more sides are equal on points, the side with the most wins will be the winner.

The Awarding of Points
a) 16 points for a win.
b) 8 points to both sides in the event of a tie.
c) If the scores are equal in a drawn match, the side batting in the fourth innings scores 8 points *plus* any bonus points scored in the first innings. First innings points are awarded only for performances *in the first 100 overs* of each first innings. They are retained whatever the result of the match.

These bonus points are as follows:
i) A maximum of four batting points:
150 to 199 runs – 1 points
200 to 249 runs – 2 points
250 to 299 runs – 3 points
300 runs or over – 4 points

ii) A maximum of four bowling points:
3 to 4 wickets taken – 1 point
5 to 6 wickets taken – 2 points
7 to 8 wickets taken – 3 points
9 to 10 wickets taken – 4 points

N.B. – If play starts when less than eight hours playing time remains, and a one innings match is played, *no* first innings bonus points can be scored. The side winning on the one innings scores 12 points.

Duration of Matches
3 days.

Hours of Play
1st and 2nd days: 11.00 a.m. – 6.30 p.m.

(or after 110 overs have been bowled, whichever is the later)
3rd day: 11.00 a.m. – 6.00 p.m.
(or after 102 overs have been bowled, whichever is the later)
There can be 30 minutes extra at the end of either the first or second days if both captains agree that there can be a definite result on that day. If they disagree, the umpires must decide. Once started this extra 30 minutes must be played out.

Covering of Pitches, Fitness of Pitches, Ground, Weather, Light
The same rules apply as for Test matches.

Intervals
Lunch – 1st and 2nd day 1.15 p.m. – 1.55 p.m.
3rd day 1 p.m. – 1.40 p.m.
Tea – 1st and 2nd day 4.10 p.m. – 4.30 p.m. or when 40 overs remain to be bowled, whichever is the later.
3rd day 3.40 p.m. – 4 p.m. or when 40 overs remain to be bowled whichever is the later.

N.B. – There are various complicated alternatives to the above timings if there have been stoppages for bad light or rain, or if an innings ends. The most important of these is that if 9 wickets are down at the time of tea, then play must continue for another half an hour, or until the last wicket falls, whichever is sooner.

Past County Champions

Year	County	Year	County
1864	Surrey	1881	Lancashire
1865	Nottinghamshire	1882	Nottinghamshire / Lancashire
1866	Middlesex		
1867	Yorkshire	1883	Nottinghamshire
1868	Nottinghamshire	1884	Nottinghamshire
1869	Nottinghamshire / Yorkshire	1885	Nottinghamshire
		1886	Nottinghamshire
1870	Yorkshire	1887	Surrey
1871	Nottinghamshire	1888	Surrey
1872	Nottinghamshire	1889	Surrey / Lancashire / Nottinghamshire
1873	Gloucestershire / Nottinghamshire		
1874	Gloucestershire	1890	Surrey
1875	Nottinghamshire	1891	Surrey
1876	Gloucestershire	1892	Surrey
1877	Gloucestershire	1893	Yorkshire
1878	Undecided	1894	Surrey
1879	Nottinghamshire / Lancashire	1895	Surrey
		1896	Yorkshire
1880	Nottinghamshire	1897	Lancashire

1898	Yorkshire	1948	Glamorgan
1899	Surrey	1949	{ Middlesex Yorkshire
1900	Yorkshire		
1901	Yorkshire	1950	{ Lancashire Surrey
1902	Yorkshire		
1903	Middlesex	1951	Warwickshire
1904	Lancashire	1952	Surrey
1905	Yorkshire	1953	Surrey
1906	Kent	1954	Surrey
1907	Nottinghamshire	1955	Surrey
1908	Yorkshire	1956	Surrey
1909	Kent	1957	Surrey
1910	Kent	1958	Surrey
1911	Warwickshire	1959	Yorkshire
1912	Yorkshire	1960	Yorkshire
1913	Kent	1961	Hampshire
1914	Surrey	1962	Yorkshire
1915–18	Not played	1963	Yorkshire
1919	Yorkshire	1964	Worcestershire
1920	Middlesex	1965	Worcestershire
1921	Middlesex	1966	Yorkshire
1922	Yorkshire	1967	Yorkshire
1923	Yorkshire	1968	Yorkshire
1924	Yorkshire	1969	Glamorgan
1925	Yorkshire	1970	Kent
1926	Lancashire	1971	Surrey
1927	Lancashire	1972	Warwickshire
1928	Lancashire	1973	Hampshire
1929	Nottinghamshire	1974	Worcestershire
1930	Lancashire	1975	Leicestershire
1931	Yorkshire	1976	Middlesex
1932	Yorkshire	1977	{ Middlesex Kent
1933	Yorkshire		
1934	Lancashire	1978	Kent
1935	Yorkshire	1979	Essex
1936	Derbyshire	1980	Middlesex
1937	Yorkshire	1981	Nottinghamshire
1938	Yorkshire	1982	Middlesex
1939	Yorkshire	1983	Essex
1940–45	Not played	1984	Essex
1946	Yorkshire	1985	Middlesex
1947	Middlesex		

3. THE NATWEST TROPHY

This competition was started in 1963 with the title of 'The Knock-out Competition'. It was sponsored by the Gillette Safety Razor Co Ltd and in 1964 the title was changed to The Gillette Cup. It remained that until 1981 when the National Westminster Bank took over the sponsorship. It is confined to the seventeen first-class counties and the thirteen leading minor counties in the previous season, along with the national teams of Scotland and Ireland.

It has attracted huge crowds ever since it began, and in addition to the sponsor's money, has brought a great deal of extra money at the gates because county members have to pay admission fees.

A Cup Final is always held at Lord's on the first Saturday of September, and is to cricket what the Cup Final at Wembley is to soccer.

This competition has not only attracted new spectators to cricket, but on the whole it has had a good influence on the game. Fielding and throwing in first-class cricket are now at their highest peak, due to the extra speed demanded of fielders in 'instant' cricket. Many batsmen too have benefited, discovering strokes they never knew they had. On the other hand it has tempted batsmen to hit across the line of the ball and to play strokes which are unorthodox and which are dangerous if they become a habit. A typical example of this is when a batsman in one-day cricket steers the ball through where the slips would normally be in first-class cricket. In the limited over game there are more often than not no slips at all. But when the batsman tries to 'steer' the ball in first-class cricket he will find slips waiting to catch him out. The other bad effect of limited over cricket is that it has encouraged the bowlers to bowl defensively, trying to prevent a batsman from scoring, rather than trying to get him out. Captains – until recently, have also been loath to put on a spin bowler, which has helped the decline in the numbers of this type of bowler.

Playing Conditions
The same as for first-class cricket in the UK except:

a) *Duration*
A match consists of one innings per side with each innings limited to 60 overs. If a match is not completed in one day, two further days are allotted.

b) No bowler may bowl more than 12 overs.

The NatWest Trophy

c) *Hours of play*
10.30 a.m. to 7.10 p.m.
The umpires may order extra time if they think a definite result can
be obtained on any day.

d) *Intervals*
Lunch 12.45 p.m. to 1.25 p.m.
Tea 20 minutes duration at either 4.30 p.m. or after 35 overs of the side batting second.
If a wicket falls in the 35th over tea will then be taken.

N.B. – For the Cup Final at Lord's every effort is made to ensure a result on the Saturday. With this in mind in the event of the match starting not less than half an hour nor more than one and a half hours late, due to the weather, each innings will be limited to 50 overs only. But if the start is delayed by *more* than one and a half hours then the 60 overs will apply and the match will almost certainly have to be continued on the Monday.

Result
In the event of a tie:

a) The side losing the lesser number of wickets is the winner.
b) If both sides are all out, the side with the higher overall scoring rate is the winner.
c) If the result cannot be decided by (a) or (b) the winner will be the side with the higher score after 30 overs, or if still equal 20 overs, or if still equal after 10 overs.

If a match remains unfinished after three days the winner is the side which has scored faster in runs per over throughout the innings, provided that at least 20 overs have been bowled at the side batting second. If the run rate is the same, the side losing the lesser number of wickets in the first 20 overs of each innings will be the winner.

Previous Winners

1963	Sussex	1975	Lancashire
1964	Sussex	1976	Northamptonshire
1965	Yorkshire	1977	Middlesex
1966	Warwickshire	1978	Sussex
1967	Kent	1979	Somerset
1968	Warwickshire	1980	Middlesex
1969	Yorkshire	1981	Derbyshire
1970	Lancashire	1982	Surrey
1971	Lancashire	1983	Somerset
1972	Lancashire	1984	Middlesex
1973	Gloucestershire	1985	Essex
1974	Kent		

4. THE BENSON & HEDGES CUP

Started in 1972 and consists of 20 teams divided into four zones. (Seventeen 1st class counties, a Minor Counties XI, a combined Oxford and Cambridge XI and Scotland).

Each team plays the others in its zone once on a league basis. The two top teams in each zone qualify to go into a draw for the quarter finals. After that the competition is played on a knock-out basis.

Points System for Zonal Matches
a) Winner – 2 points
b) In a 'no result' match 1 point to each team
In the event of two or more teams in any one zone having an equal number of points, their positions will be based on the faster rate of taking wickets in all zone matches.

Playing Conditions
55 overs for each side – No bowler may bowl more than 11 overs.

Hours of Play
11 a.m. – 7 p.m.
Lunch – 1.15 p.m. – 1.55 p.m.
Tea – 20 mins – at 4.30 p.m. or after 35 overs of the side batting second whichever is the later.
Duration – Three days allotted.

Result
Conditions as for the NatWest Trophy.

Previous Winners

1972	Leicestershire	1979	Essex
1973	Kent	1980	Northamptonshire
1974	Surrey	1981	Somerset
1975	Leicestershire	1982	Somerset
1976	Kent	1983	Middlesex
1977	Gloucestershire	1984	Lancashire
1978	Kent	1985	Leicestershire

5. THE JOHN PLAYER LEAGUE

This competition started in 1969 and was unashamedly a copy of the Gillette Cup, but with certain differences to suit Sunday play. In the early and mid-sixties BBC2 televised a weekly Sunday match played by the International Cavaliers – a team made up of past and present Test players from all the countries. The great success of these games

The John Player League Trophy.

encouraged the TCCB to begin the present John Player League for the 17 first-class counties.

Playing Conditions
a) *Hours of Play*
Normally 2.00 p.m. – 7.00 p.m. with a tea interval of 20 minutes at the end of the over in progress at 4.20 p.m., or between innings whichever is the earlier. The duration and time of the tea interval can be varied in the case of a match interrupted by weather. Close of play will *normally* be at 7.00 p.m. but play may continue after that time if in the opinion of the umpires, the overs remaining to be bowled can be completed by 7.10 p.m. If the match is being televised, hours of play are 1.30 p.m. – 6.30 p.m. with a tea interval at 3.50 p.m. – 4.10 p.m.

b) *Length of Innings – in an uninterrupted Match*
i) Each team will bat for 40 overs unless all out earlier.
ii) In the event of the team fielding first failing to bowl 40 overs by 4.10 p.m., the over in progress will be completed and the innings of the team batting second will be limited to the same number of overs as the innings of the team batting first.

c) If the team batting first is all out and its last wicket falls within two minutes of the scheduled time for tea, the innings of the side batting second will be limited to the same number of overs as the innings of the team batting first.
   In matches where the start is delayed the number of overs will be arranged so that both teams have the opportunity of batting the same number of overs (minimum – 10 overs each team). The calculation of the number of overs to be bowled is based on the average rate of 18 overs per hour (one over per $3\frac{1}{3}$ minutes).
   There are other regulations regarding the number of overs to be bowled due to interference by the weather, but they are far too complicated for me to try to explain!

Result
In matches where both teams have had the opportunity of batting the same number of overs, the team scoring the higher number of runs is the winner. But if the scores are equal the result is a tie *and no account will be taken of the number of wickets which have fallen.*

Points
4 for a win

2 each for a tie
2 each in a 'No Result' match.

At the end of the season if two or more teams finish with an equal number of points for any of the first four places, their final positions will be decided by:

a) The most wins, or if still equal,

b) The most *away* wins, or if still equal,

c) The higher run rate throughout the season (to be calculated by runs scored divided by balls bowled, excluding wides and no balls.

Previous Winners

1969	Lancashire	1977	Leicestershire
1970	Lancashire	1978	Hampshire
1971	Worcestershire	1979	Somerset
1972	Kent	1980	Warwickshire
1973	Kent	1981	Essex
1974	Leicestershire	1982	Sussex
1975	Hampshire	1983	Yorkshire
1976	Kent	1984	Essex
		1985	Essex

6. THE MINOR COUNTY CHAMPIONSHIP

First formed in 1895 and is made up of counties not considered good enough to be first-class. From time to time minor counties *do* apply to enter the first-class County Championship. Glamorgan did so in 1921, and Devon, Northumberland and Durham have all toyed with the idea. But it's not just the question of having a team of sufficiently high standard. Lack of the necessary finance is the chief problem and not surprisingly so when it takes anything up to a million pounds a year to run a first-class county.

Nowadays the Championship consists of twenty sides – the 19 minor counties plus Somerset 2nd XI. They are divided into an Eastern and Western Division. All teams play nine matches and the winners of each Division then meet in a 55 overs a side one day game to decide the Championship. This game is played at Worcester.

The nine games in the Division are of two days duration, with two innings a side. Points are awarded as follows:

a) For a win – 10 points.

b) In a drawn match the side which is ahead after 55 overs of the 1st innings gets 3 points, and the other side 1 point.

c) If the match is abandoned with no result each side gets 2 points.

d) There is also a knock-out competition of 55 overs a side between the 19 minor counties. The final of this is played at the ground of one of the finalists.

Previous Minor County Champions

1895	Norfolk Durham Worcestershire	1934	Lancashire 2nd
		1935	Middlesex 2nd
		1936	Hertfordshire
1896	Worcestershire	1937	Lancashire 2nd
1897	Worcestershire	1938	Buckinghamshire
1898	Worcestershire	1939	Surrey 2nd
1899	Northamptonshire Buckinghamshire	1946	Suffolk
		1947	Yorkshire 2nd
1900	Glamorgan Durham Northamptonshire	1948	Lancashire 2nd
		1949	Lancashire 2nd
		1950	Surrey 2nd
1901	Durham	1951	Kent 2nd
1902	Wiltshire	1952	Buckinghamshire
1903	Northamptonshire	1953	Berkshire
1904	Northamptonshire	1954	Surrey 2nd
1905	Norfolk	1955	Surrey 2nd
1906	Staffordshire	1956	Kent 2nd
1907	Lancashire 2nd	1957	Yorkshire 2nd
1908	Staffordshire	1958	Yorkshire 2nd
1909	Wiltshire	1959	Warwickshire 2nd
1910	Norfolk	1960	Lancashire 2nd
1911	Staffordshire	1961	Somerset 2nd
1912	In abeyance	1962	Warwickshire 2nd
1913	Norfolk	1963	Cambridgeshire
1920	Staffordshire	1964	Lancashire 2nd
1921	Staffordshire	1965	Somerset 2nd
1922	Buckinghamshire	1966	Lincolnshire
1923	Buckinghamshire	1967	Cheshire
1924	Berkshire	1968	Yorkshire 2nd
1925	Buckinghamshire	1969	Buckinghamshire
1926	Durham	1970	Bedfordshire
1927	Staffordshire	1971	Yorkshire 2nd
1928	Berkshire	1972	Bedfordshire
1929	Oxfordshire	1973	Shropshire
1930	Durham	1974	Oxfordshire
1931	Leicestershire 2nd	1975	Hertfordshire
1932	Buckinghamshire	1976	Durham
1933	Undecided	1977	Suffolk

1978	Devon	1982	Oxfordshire
1979	Suffolk	1983	Hertfordshire
1980	Durham	1984	Durham
1981	Durham	1985	Cheshire

7. LEAGUE CRICKET

Matches in these leagues, to be found in the North, Midlands, Scotland and Wales are played on Saturdays and Sundays or in the evenings during mid-week. Some are played on a limited-over basis, others with a normal one innings a side.

8. WILLIAM YOUNGER CLUB CRICKET CHAMPIONSHIP CUP

This competition was started in 1969 by Derrick Robins in conjunction with *The Cricketer*; in 1976 it was sponsored by John Haig and organized by the National Cricket Association. Since 1983 it has become the William Younger Cup. It's for Cricket Clubs★ and is played under NatWest rules but with 45 overs instead of 60, and with each bowler restricted to a maximum of 9 overs.

The competition is open to all Cricket Clubs that are affiliated to the National Cricket Association. All players must be members of the Club at the beginning of the season. A professional cricketer can NOT play unless he is a registered first-class cricketer who has played only *one* game for his county in the current season in any of the competitions.

Previous Winners

1969	Hampstead	1978	Cheltenham
1970	Cheltenham	1979	Scarborough
1971	Blackheath	1980	Moseley
1972	Scarborough	1981	Scarborough
1973	Wolverhampton	1982	Scarborough
1974	Sunbury	1983	Shrewsbury
1975	York	1984	Old Hill
1976	Scarborough	1985	Old Hill
1977	Southgate		

★ To qualify a club must have a recognized home and away week-end fixture list, and play on a home ground of suitable standard.

9. THE CRICKETER CUP AND MOËT AND CHANDON AWARD

A knock-out competition for Public School Old Boys' Teams. It started in 1967 when sixteen schools were invited to play. In 1969 a further sixteen schools were invited to compete, and thirty-two teams have entered ever since. The final is played in London either at Burton's Court in Chelsea, or at Vincent Square in Westminster. This is a splendid social occasion with the winners not only getting the award but a day's visit to the Moët and Chandon Château at Epernay in France.

Playing Conditions
55 overs each innings with each bowler limited to a maximum of 12 overs.

Previous Winners

1967	Repton	1977	Shrewsbury
1968	Malvern	1978	Charterhouse
1969	Brighton	1979	Tonbridge
1970	Winchester	1980	Marlborough
1971	Tonbridge	1981	Charterhouse
1972	Tonbridge	1982	Winchester
1973	Rugby	1983	Repton
1974	Winchester	1984	Tonbridge
1975	Malvern	1985	Oundle
1976	Tonbridge		

10. THE NORSK HYDRO FERTILISER VILLAGE CRICKET CHAMPIONSHIP

This is a limited over zonal knock-out competition for villages. It is organized by *The Cricketer* and first took place in 1972. It has been sponsored by Haig, Whitbread and now from 1986 by Norsk Hydro Fertilisers. In 1985, 639 villages entered the competition. The definition of a village is a rural community surrounded by open country on *all* sides, and with a population of not more than 2,500. Villages entering are required to pay a subscription to *The Cricketer*. A village is not eligible to enter in any season in which it plays in the William Younger Cup.

A player must be a paid-up member of the club and have played at least eight matches for the village in the last three years.

The normal laws of cricket and one-day rules apply with 40 overs for each innings and no bowler allowed to bowl more than 9 overs.

The Final is a great occasion and is always played at Lord's on a

Sunday at the end of August or at the beginning of September. Crowds of six thousand or more attend which is proof of the popularity of the competition in villages throughout the country.

Previous Winners

1972	Troon	1979	East Brierley
1973	Troon	1980	Marchwiel
1974	Bomarsund	1981	St Fagans
1975	Gowerton	1982	St Fagans
1976	Troon	1983	Quarundon
1977	Cookley	1984	Marchwiel
1978	Linton Park	1985	Freuchie

11. INTERNATIONAL MATCHES INCLUDING THE WORLD CUP

There have now been three World Cups all sponsored by the Prudential Assurance Company. The winners have been West Indies – 1975, West Indies – 1979 and India – 1983. Prudential also sponsored the one-day Internationals between England and the visiting touring teams – 3 matches being played. The above sponsorship has now been taken over by Texaco Ltd and the teams compete for the Texaco Trophy. Conditions of play are as for other one day matches – 55 overs per side – 11 overs maximum allowed to each bowler – Normal hours of play 10.45 a.m. – 7.15 p.m.

The result of a tied match to stand unless it is necessary to declare a winner of the match in order to decide the series. In which case the winner is:

a) The side losing the lesser number of wickets.

b) If both sides are all out, the side with the higher overall scoring rate.

c) If the result cannot be decided by either of these then it is the side with the higher score after 30 overs, or 20 overs or if still equal 10 overs.

N.B. – The next World Cup will be held in India and Pakistan in 1987. Due to short evenings each match will be 60 overs per innings and will be scheduled for *two* days, not one.

GENERAL RULES AND PLAYING CONDITIONS FOR ALL LIMITED OVER COMPETITIONS

1. The matches are *not* considered first-class.

2. No declarations may be made at any time.

3. At the instant of delivery a minimum of four fielders (plus the bowler and wicket-keeper) must be within an area bounded by two semi-circles centred on each middle stump – each with a radius of 30 yards, and joined by a parallel line on each side of the pitch. In the event of an infringement the square leg umpire must call 'No Ball'.

4. If a player has to leave the field for medical attention due to an injury caused by an external blow (e.g. *not* a pulled muscle) he may bowl immediately on his return to the field.

5. No bowler may deliver the ball under-arm.

6. No bowler may bowl more than one fifth of the allocated overs.

7. Umpires are instructed to apply a very strict interpretation in regard to the bowling of wides. This is to prevent deliberate bowling wide of the wicket or over the batsman's head.

The Ashes

TWO OF THE most thrilling moments of my broadcasting life have been the two occasions when I was lucky enough to be the commentator when England regained the Ashes in 1953 and 1971. Sadly for me in 1977 when England regained the Ashes again at Headingley I just missed doing the hat trick! I was due to take up the commentary the next over from Christopher Martin-Jenkins, the BBC cricket correspondent.

But on 19 August 1953 I was the commentator on television at the Oval when Denis Compton swept Arthur Morris for four to the gas holders, and the BBC still play the recording of my jubilant and excited cry: 'It's the Ashes, it's the Ashes!'.

Eighteen years later on 17 February 1971, I was on the radio in Australia at the moment when Ray Illingworth's England team regained the Ashes at Sydney. BBC Radio 2 had stayed open throughout the night and from what I have heard since, this exciting moment of cricket history was heard by listeners all over the cricketing world at varying times of the day and night . . . 'Underwood to Jenner, Jenner snicks it on to his pad, Fletcher has caught it at silly point, he's caught it, England have won back the Ashes after twelve years and the England team are chairing their captain, Illingworth, off the field . . .'.

These were the words I used at the time and how proud and lucky I felt to be on the air just then. It is an emotional moment – this winning of the Ashes – especially after touring round with a team and sharing all its triumphs and disasters.

Some people think that the Ashes are to blame for a lot of the slow play and safety-first tactics we see during an England v. Australia series. They reason that the side holding the Ashes has only to draw the series to keep them and so is tempted to take few risks in order to win. There is certainly some truth in this and some captains have said that they would be in favour of fighting each series separately and doing away with the Ashes. But I believe on balance that it is better to keep things as they are. The Ashes are part of cricket history and cricket is a game of tradition.

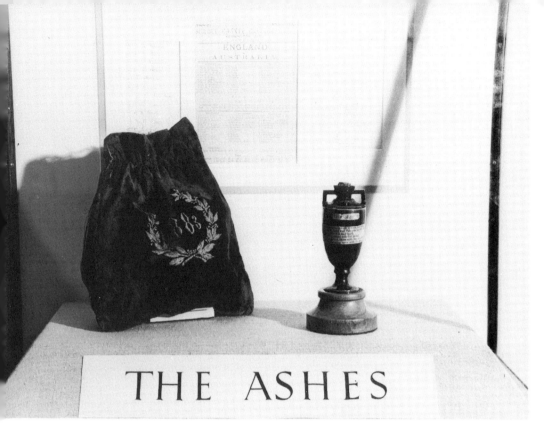

THE ASHES

What exactly are the Ashes and how did they come about? The Ashes are to cricket what the World Cup is to football, or the Derby to horse-racing. 'They' are the supreme challenge and the most coveted of all cricket trophies and yet they can only be won by two of the cricketing countries, England or Australia. Their origin goes back to August 1882 when Australia beat England by 7 runs at the Oval and so won their first Test victory in England. On the following day the *Sporting Times* published a mock obituary for English cricket as follows:

In affectionate remembrance
of
English Cricket
which died at the Oval 29th August 1882
deeply lamented by a large circle of sorrowing
friends and acquaintances
R.I.P.
N.B. The body will be cremated and
the Ashes taken to Australia

In the following winter (1882–83) the Hon. Ivo Bligh took a team to Australia and won two of the three Test matches played. At the end of the third match some ladies burnt a bail and sealed the Ashes in a small urn and presented it to the England captain, later the 8th Earl of Darnley. The urn remained his private property until his death in 1927 when it was bequeathed to MCC and is now kept in the Imperial Cricket Memorial Gallery at the back of the Pavilion at Lord's. The Ashes therefore exist but, although played for, never leave Lord's.

The Ashes have been won and held as follows:

Season	Won by	Location	Held for
1882–83*	Australia	Australia	1 year
1884	England	England	7 years
1891–92	Australia	Australia	1 year
1893	England	England	4 years
1897–98	Australia	Australia	6 years
1903–4	England	Australia	3 years
1907–8	Australia	Australia	4 years
1911–12	England	Australia	8 years
1920–22	Australia	Australia	5 years
1926	England	England	4 years
1930	Australia	England	3 years
1932–33	England	Australia	1 year
1934	Australia	England	19 years
1953	England	England	5 years
1958–59	Australia	Australia	12 years
1970–71	England	Australia	3 years
1974–75	Australia	Australia	2 years
1977	England	England	3 years
1979–80	Australia	Australia	1 year
1981	England	England	2 years
1982–83	Australia	Australia	2 years
1985	England	England	???

* After Bligh had defeated Murdoch's Australians 2–1 in the scheduled 3-match series, an extra match was played – and lost – against a stronger, combined Australian team. This has to be treated as a separate 'series' otherwise the Ashes would have never been Bligh's.

On their return to England in March 1971 the whole MCC team recorded a song on Decca F13175 entitled 'The Ashes Song'. The music is a traditional old music hall tune, the original words of which were 'Show me your Winkle Tonight'! After the Ashes had been won we put new words to this tune and here they are:

THE ASHES SONG

We've brought the Ashes back home
We've got them here in the urn
The Aussies had had them twelve years
So it was about our turn
But Oh! what a tough fight
It's been in the dazzling sunlight
In spite of the boos of the mob on the Hill
We've won by two matches to nil

When we arrived people said
The Aussies would leave us for dead
But we knew we would prove them wrong
And that's why we're singing this song
But oh! the feeling is great
For losing is something we hate
So Sydney we thank you for both of our wins
But not for those bottles and tins

Our openers gave us a good start
And the others then all played their part
We usually made a good score
Seven times three hundred or more
The Aussies however were apt
To collapse at the drop of a hat
If they were bowled any ball that was short
It was ten to one on they'd be caught

In the field it was often too hot
So sometimes we felt very low
Whether rain was forecast or not
We always knew we'd have Snow
So now to go home we are free
And we're sure the Aussies agree
Though the series has been a long uphill climb
We've all had a real bumper time

HOW'S THAT!

15 August 1977 at Headingley was an equally magic moment when Derek Randall caught a skier at cover, turned a somersault, and England had regained the Ashes under their new captain Mike Brearley in his first Test series as captain. What a wonderful way for

cricket to celebrate the Queen's Silver Jubilee! And by an amazing coincidence 1926 when Percy Chapman's team regained the Ashes at the Oval was the year of the Queen's birth, and Len Hutton's triumph in 1953 was in Coronation Year. So there is now a decided aura of royalty surrounding the Ashes.

1985 brought further rejoicing for England supporters when Gower's team regained the Ashes at the Oval, winning the series 3–1.

Test Matches - Six of the Best

TEST MATCHES are played between *full* members of the International Cricket Conference. The first ever Test was played at Melbourne between Australia and England on 15th, 16th, 17th March 1877. Since South Africa left the Imperial Cricket Conference in 1961, Tests between them and England, Australia and New Zealand were *un*official, but have been included in Test match records in Wisden and all other statistical books. The matches England played against the Rest of the World in 1970 were also considered to be *un*official Tests at the time, and at first were included in Test match records. But subsequently the records of players who played in those Rest of the World matches, have been separated from Test match records.

Tests were originally of three days' duration but can in fact be any length of three days or over as agreed between the two countries playing. For instance in Australia between the wars, tests were played to a finish; others in England have been four days, and there was the famous *timeless* Test at Durban in 1939 which ended in a draw after ten days because MCC had to catch the boat home!

Laws and regulations for Test matches are in general the same as for first-class matches, though the two countries playing may agree to certain amendments – the home country usually laying down the conditions. For instance on MCC's last tour of South Africa in 1964–65 the follow-on deficit was 150 runs instead of 200, even though the Tests were of five days' duration. Again when MCC were in West Indies in 1967–68 there was *no* limit to the number of fielders allowed *behind* the popping crease on the leg-side. Here in England in recent years, the TCCB has tried to insist on a regulation which says that a minimum of ninety overs must be bowled during a day's play, but not all visiting sides have agreed. Australia refused in 1981, and West Indies in 1984. But in 1985 Australia did agree, and as a result – even in a rainy season, spectators got their money's worth.

For the results of Test matches between the 8 countries see page 215.

I am now going to choose what I consider to have been the six best

51

out of the 225 Test matches on which I have commentated since 1946. I'm going to cheat a bit, though. As the hors-d'oeuvre I must include one at which I did not commentate. But how I wish that I had been there! I refer to the one and only tie ever to have happened in Test cricket – Australia v. West Indies at Brisbane in 1960.

In view of its fairy-tale finish perhaps the most remarkable thing about it was that up to noon on the last day it was just a very good game of cricket which, it seemed, after a hard struggle, Australia would win fairly easily. West Indies won the toss and batted first, making 453 with Sobers scoring a magnificent 132. Australia replied with 505 of which O'Neill made 181 – his biggest Test score – supported by Bobbie Simpson with 92. In West Indies' second innings, Alan Davidson, who had taken 5 wickets for Australia in the first innings, again bowled superbly and thanks largely to his taking another 6 wickets West Indies were all out for 284 after half an hour's play on the fifth and final day of the match. This meant that Australia only had to score 233 to win at a rate of about 45 runs per hour – an easy task on paper even though Wes Hall did take a long time to bowl his overs.

They started disastrously, losing Simpson and Harvey for a mere 7 runs, and soon after lunch they were 57 for 5 with O'Neill, McDonald, and Favell all out. A stand of 35 between Mackay and Davidson took the score to 92 for 6 when Mackay was bowled by Ramadhin, and the Australian captain, Benaud, joined Davidson with only Grout, Meckiff, and Kline to come. The odds had swung West Indies' way. At tea, the score was 110 for 6 and Australia needed 123 to win at a run a minute with 4 wickets in hand – quite possible, but it still looked like a West Indies victory. Davidson and Benaud thought otherwise. They hit the bad balls for 4 and ran like stags between the wickets, turning ones into twos and half runs into quick singles. The game swung completely Australia's way and with 10 minutes to go they needed only 9 runs to win with Davidson and Benaud still going strong. It then looked as if Australia had this first Test in the bag. But now – as they say – read on!

Sobers bowled a ball down the leg-side to Benaud who pushed it for a single – 8 to win. Davidson took another run off Sobers and so gave Benaud the strike – 7 to win. Another ball pitched on the leg stump and Benaud thought he would pinch another quick run by pushing it wide of Joe Solomon at forward square leg. But as he called for one and ran, Solomon threw in from side-on and hit the stumps with Davidson a yard out at the wicket-keeper's end. So Davidson was run out for his highest score in Test cricket – a fine 80 – and Australia with 3 wickets in hand still needed 7 runs to win.

Wally Grout came in, played two balls from Sobers and then scored a single off the seventh ball of Sobers' over. Six to win and with Benaud failing to score off the last ball of the over, Grout was left at the striker's end to face Hall in what was certain to be the last over of the match as there were now only 4 minutes to go.

Hall went slowly back to his mark to start his long run – at that time by far the longest in the world. It was obviously essential for Grout to give Benaud the strike and as the first ball struck him somewhere on the body, the ball dropped at his feet and Benaud scampered up the pitch with Grout in considerable pain somehow reaching safety at the other end.

Five to win. Seven balls to go and Hall proceeded to bowl a very fast bumper which Benaud tried to hook for 4 and so level the scores. But the ball hit his glove and he was well caught behind the wicket by Gerry Alexander. Benaud out for a captain's 52, still 5 runs to make for victory, now only 6 balls left and Ian Meckiff – no great shakes as a batsman – the next man in. He played the first ball without scoring, and missed the second which went through to Alexander standing a long way back. Grout, backing up, called Meckiff and they just managed a bye, with Alexander returning the ball quickly to Hall who threw it, but missed the stumps at the bowler's end. Four runs to win, with 4 balls left. Hall next bowled a good length ball to Grout and it flew off the top edge of his bat to Kanhai at backward square leg. But to the horror of every West Indian present, Wes Hall following through fast, dashed for the catch himself and missed what would have been an easy enough catch for Kanhai. The batsman had taken one run, so now it was 3 balls to go and 3 runs to win. Meckiff hit the next ball from Hall up in the air over mid-wicket and it looked a certain four and victory for Australia. But the grass in the outfield had not been mown that day and Conrad Hunte ran round the boundary and was able to pick up the ball which stopped a foot or so from the boundary. The batsmen had run two and were going for the third which would win the match, but in one fell swoop, Hunte picked up the ball and threw it 80 yards straight over the top of the stumps to Alexander. Grout flung himself at the crease but he was out – by a cat's whisker.

What a throw! What speed and accuracy! Just imagine the excitement. As the batsmen had run 2, the scores were now level and one run was wanted for victory by Australia with two balls to go. This was Hall's eighteenth over of the innings and he must have been almost dropping. But he tore up to the bowling crease and bowled a fast one on the stumps to Kline who pushed it to forward short leg and ran. Once again Solomon was the fielder and once

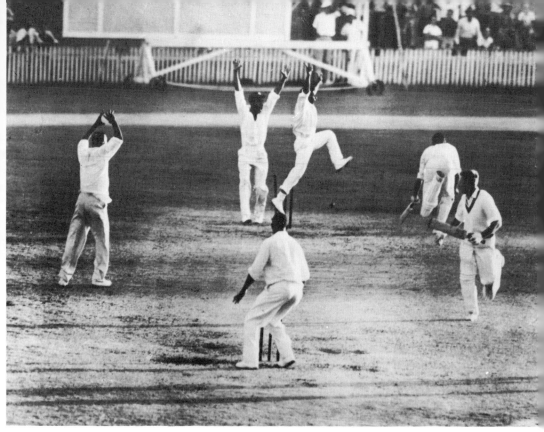

The run out of Ian Meckiff which caused
the First Test to end in a tie.

again – incredible to relate – he picked up and threw down the stumps from side-on with Meckiff just short of the crease. A roar, and up went the umpire's finger. Possibly the greatest, certainly the most exciting Test match had finished in a tie and I doubt if any of the twenty-two players would have wished for any other result.

FIRST TEST MATCH
Played at Brisbane, 9, 10, 12, 13 and 14 December
Match tied

WEST INDIES

C C Hunte	c Benaud b Davidson	24	c Simpson b Mackay	39
C W Smith	c Grout b Davidson	7	c O'Neill b Davidson	6
R B Kanhai	c Grout b Davidson	15	c Grout b Davidson	54
G S Sobers	c Kline b Meckiff	132	b Davidson	14
†F M M Worrell	c Grout b Davidson	65	c Grout b Davidson	65
J S Solomon	hit wkt b Simpson	65	lbw b Simpson	47
P D Lashley	c Grout b Kline	19	b Davidson	0
‡F C M Alexander	c Davidson b Kline	60	b Benaud	5
S Ramadhin	c Harvey b Davidson	12	c Harvey b Simpson	6
W W Hall	st Grout b Kline	50	b Davidson	18
A L Valentine	not out	0	not out	7
Extras	(lb 3, w 1)	4	(b 14, lb 7, w 2)	23
Total		453		284

AUSTRALIA

	1st innings		2nd innings	
C C McDonald	c Hunte b Sobers	57	b Worrell	16
R B Simpson	b Ramadhin	92	c sub b Hall	0
R N Harvey	b Valentine	15	c Sobers b Hall	5
N C O'Neill	c Valentine b Hall	181	c Alexander b Hall	26
L E Favell	run out	45	c Solomon b Hall	7
K D Mackay	b Sobers	35	b Ramadhin	28
A K Davidson	c Alexander b Hall	44	run out	80
†R Benaud	lbw b Hall	10	c Alexander b Hall	52
‡A T W Grout	lbw b Hall	4	run out	2
I W Meckiff	run out	4	run out	2
L F Kline	not out	3	not out	0
Extras	(b 2, lb 8, nb 4, w 1)	15	(b 2, lb 9, nb 3)	14
Total		505		232

BOWLING

AUSTRALIA	O	M	R	W	O	M	R	W
Davidson	30	2	135	5	24.6	4	87	6
Meckiff	18	0	129	1	4	1	19	0
Mackay	3	0	15	0	21	7	52	1
Benaud	24	3	93	0	31	6	69	1
Simpson	8	0	25	1	7	2	18	2
Kline	17.6	6	52	3	4	0	14	0
O'Neill					1	0	2	0
WEST INDIES								
Hall	29.3	1	140	4	17.7	3	63	5
Worrell	30	0	93	0	16	3	41	1
Sobers	32	0	115	2	8	0	30	0
Valentine	24	6	82	1	10	4	27	0
Ramadhin	15	1	60	1	17	3	57	1

FALL OF WICKETS

	WI 1st	A 1st	WI 2nd	A 2nd
1st	23	84	13	1
2nd	42	138	88	7
3rd	65	194	114	49
4th	239	278	127	49
5th	243	381	210	57
6th	283	469	210	92
7th	347	484	241	226
8th	366	489	250	228
9th	452	496	253	232
10th	453	505	284	232

Umpires: C J Edgar and C Hoy

† Captain ‡ Wicket-keeper

ENGLAND *v.* AUSTRALIA – THE OVAL, 1953

Whenever I am asked which is my most memorable moment in Test cricket I invariably choose the last ball of the final Test between England and Australia at the Oval in 1953. The first four Tests had all been drawn but in this fifth and final Test, England, under a professional captain in Coronation year, won the match and the series and so regained the Ashes which Australia had held since 1934 – a period of nineteen years. As you can imagine, there were tremendous scenes of enthusiasm at the end of the game. I shall never forget the sight of Edrich and Compton fighting their way back to the pavilion through the converging crowd, though in fact it was only possible to follow their progress from their bats held aloft rather like two submarine periscopes.

For the fifth time in the series, Australia's captain, Hassett, won the toss, and England went into the field with an extra bowler – May and Trueman coming in for two batsmen, Watson and Simpson. But in spite of the Oval pitch's reputation for taking spin, Australia left out Benaud and had no genuine spinner in their side, something which later they were to regret.

Right from the start Bedser and Trueman bowled superbly and, helped by two showers which freshened up the pitch, soon had half the Australian side out for 118. But thanks to some splendid big hitting by Ray Lindwall, who made 62, Australia recovered and their last 5 wickets added 157 to give them a total of 275. England batted for 2 overs in the first evening before bad light stopped play. Hutton was nearly out off a bouncer from Lindwall. He snicked it on to his cap which slowed it down so that it dropped short of the slips. But in the process it knocked off his cap, which nearly hit the stumps, when, of course, he would have been out 'hit wicket'.

On the second day – Monday – England fared badly against Lindwall and Johnston, and in spite of a typical 82 from Hutton and a useful 39 from May, they finished with 235 for 7 with Bailey fighting back. Next morning, supported first by Trueman, then by Bedser, Bailey went on to make 64 and thanks to a last wicket partnership of 44 between him and Bedser, England finished 31 runs ahead.

This proved to Hutton that the pitch was growing easier and would no longer help the quicker bowlers. So when Australia went in and had only scored 19 runs, Hutton brought on his famous Surrey spinners, Laker and Lock. From that moment on Australia were in terrible trouble. An hour later they had lost 5 wickets for 61, only 30 runs ahead, thanks to Lock's great accuracy and Laker's spin. Ron Archer with a thrilling 49 tried to hit them out of trouble with a 6 and seven 4s but the innings ended with the score at 162, Lock and Laker taking 5 and 4 wickets respectively. With three possible days and 50 minutes left for play (a sixth day could be used if necessary) England needed only 132 to win. Hutton was run out going for a second run when the score was 24 but at the close of play Edrich and May were still together and England needed only 94 to regain the Ashes.

There was tremendous tension and excitement on that last morning at the Oval and the runs came extremely slowly – only 24 in the first hour. Then, with the score at 88, May was out and in came Denis Compton to join his Middlesex 'twin' Bill Edrich. Slowly they added 35 runs and then at about a quarter to three Hassett conceded defeat by putting himself on to bowl. Four runs were scored off his over and so with 5 runs needed he called to his vice-captain, Arthur Morris, to bowl his slow left-arm chinamen from the Pavilion end. A single to Edrich, then Compton played the next two balls with exaggerated care – the crowd were on tenterhooks and they shouted encouragement and crowded round the boundary edge waiting to rush on to the field.

Then Morris bowled one of his off-spinners outside the leg stump. I was commentating on television at the time. 'This is it!' I thought, as I saw Compton play his famous sweep. But no! He hit it all right but the ball was magnificently fielded by Alan Davidson at backward short-leg. Loud cheers and groans – the uproar was now continuous. The fifth ball was the same as the previous one – a slow off-break outside the leg stump. This time Compton made no mistake and hit the ball hard down towards the gas-holders. Whether it ever got there I don't think anyone knows – ball and fielders were enveloped by the crowd and up in our television box, overcome by excitement and emotion, I was only able to shout hoarsely 'It's the Ashes, it's the Ashes.' By bowling those last five balls, Arthur Morris became the most televised Test bowler ever! From then on they were used as a demonstration film sequence in every TV and radio shop in the land and were played for hour after hour, day after day. Such is fame!

FIFTH TEST MATCH
At the Oval, 15, 17, 18, 19, 20 and 21 August
England won in four days by 8 wickets

AUSTRALIA

†A L Hassett	c Evans b Bedser	53	lbw b Laker	10
A R Morris	lbw b Bedser	16	lbw b Lock	26
K R Miller	lbw b Bailey	1	c Trueman b Laker	0
R N Harvey	c Hutton b Trueman	36	b Lock	1
G B Hole	c Evans b Trueman	37	lbw b Laker	17
J H de Courcy	c Evans b Trueman	5	run out	4
R G Archer	c and b Bedser	10	c Edrich b Lock	49
A K Davidson	c Edrich b Laker	22	b Lock	21
R R Lindwall	c Evans b Trueman	62	c Compton b Laker	12
‡G R A Langley	c Edrich b Lock	18	c Trueman b Lock	2
W A Johnston	not out	9	not out	6
Extras	(b 4, nb 2)	6	(b 11, lb 3)	14
Total		275		162

ENGLAND

†L Hutton	b Johnston	82	run out	17
W J Edrich	lbw b Lindwall	21	not out	55
P B H May	c Archer b Johnston	39	c Davidson b Miller	37
D C S Compton	c Langley b Lindwall	16	not out	22
T W Graveney	c Miller b Lindwall	4		
T E Bailey	b Archer	64		
‡T G Evans	run out	28		
J C Laker	c Langley b Miller	1		
G A R Lock	c Davidson b Lindwall	4		
F S Trueman	b Johnston	10		
A V Bedser	not out	22		
Extras	(b 9, lb 5, w 1)	15	(lb 1	1
Total		306	(for 2 wkts)	132

		BOWLING								FALL OF WICKETS			
ENGLAND	O	M	R	W	O	M	R	W		A	E	A	E
										1st	*1st*	*2nd*	*2nd*
Bedser	29	3	88	3	11	2	24	0	1st	38	37	23	24
Trueman	24.3	3	86	4	2	1	4	0	2nd	41	137	59	88
Bailey	14	3	42	1					3rd	107	154	60	
Lock	9	2	19	1	21	9	45	5	4th	107	167	61	
Laker	5	0	34	1	16.5	2	75	4	5th	118	170	61	
AUSTRALIA									6th	160	210	85	
Lindwall	32	7	70	4	21	5	46	0	7th	160	225	135	
Miller	34	12	65	1	11	3	24	1	8th	207	237	140	
Johnston	45	16	94	3	29	14	52	0	9th	245	262	144	
Davidson	10	1	26	0					10th	275	306	162	
Archer	10.3	2	25	1	1	1	0	0					
Hole	11	6	11	0									
Hassett					1	0	4	0					
Morris					0.5	0	5	0					

† Captain   ‡ Wicket-keeper

Umpires: D Davies and F S Lee

ENGLAND v. WEST INDIES – LORD'S, 1963

I shall never forget the dramatic climax of the second Test at Lord's in 1963 between England and the West Indies. At the BBC it is famous as the Test which stopped the TV News – literally. Because of the tremendous excitement at the finish I was told by our producer to say that we would stay at Lord's and not go over to Alexandra Palace for the usual 5.50 news – something quite unheard of at the BBC where the News is sacred. In fact someone up at Alexandra Palace must have had itchy fingers or perhaps disliked or knew nothing about cricket, for after listening to an over of commentary and not getting the finish they had expected, they quietly faded us and started the News – only to be swamped by telephone calls from irate viewers, one of whom happened to be the Director of BBC TV himself. So back they hurriedly came and viewers were able to share in one of the most thrilling finishes ever.

But right from the start the match was a winner – first one side was on top, then the other and so it went on for five days. England brought back Derek Shackleton at the age of thirty-eight and, captained by Ted Dexter, lost the toss. Frank Worrell chose to bat and Conrad Hunte hit the first three balls of the match off Freddie Trueman for 4 apiece. What a start! Poor Freddie was perhaps handicapped by a slippery run-up as rain had delayed the start. But for the rest of the day England were on top. At lunch the West Indies' score was only 47, Shackleton moving the ball all over the place but without any luck. Kanhai played attractively for 73, and Sobers, 42, and Solomon, 56, shared useful stands with him. But at the close of play West Indies were only 245 for 6, 5 of the wickets falling to Trueman, none to the unlucky Shackleton. But he made up for it the next morning, taking 3 wickets in 4 balls to finish off the West Indies' innings for a total of 301.

58

Then Charlie Griffith struck two early blows for West Indies and with Edrich and Stewart out, England were 20 for 2 when Ken Barrington joined Ted Dexter. There followed a masterful display of power-driving and hooking by Ted Dexter. He lashed the fiery fast bowling all over the field. He reached his 50 in 48 minutes and hit ten 4s in 81 minutes off 73 balls before being lbw to Sobers for 70. I give these details because for me this is still the best short Test innings I have ever seen. Dexter and Barrington had added 82 in an hour. But Cowdrey and Close failed and it was left to Barrington's 80 and Parks' 35 to help England to 244 for 7 at close of play. The pattern was much the same as the West Indies' innings on the day before. But in spite of a brave 52 not out by Freddie Titmus England were all out for 297 on the Saturday morning, 4 runs behind and with Charlie Griffith finishing with bowling figures of 5 for 91.

At the start of West Indies' second innings the game swung right round once more in England's favour, Trueman and Shackleton dismissing five West Indies' batsmen for 104. Surely England were on top now? Yes, but by the close of play a fine partnership by Basil Butcher and Frank Worrell took the West Indies' score to 214 for 5 – a more than useful lead of 218 in a match where the bowlers were on top of the batsmen. But on Monday morning the see-saw started again and West Indies' innings closed for 229 – the last 5 wickets falling for only 15 runs in 6 overs. Butcher made a great 133 and he and Worrell had added 110. Once again Trueman had done most of the damage, taking 5 for 52, giving him 11 for 152 in the match, supported by Shackleton with figures of 4 for 72.

So with just under 11½ hours left to play, England needed 234 to win. Although such a total wouldn't be reached without a fight, there was all the time in the world and at this point English hopes were high. But as happened so often in this match they were soon to be dashed. Stewart, Edrich, and Dexter were quickly out and England were 31 for 3, leaving 203 runs still needed when Cowdrey joined Barrington. Hall was bowling very fast and short and the ball was lifting dangerously. The two batsmen stuck it bravely but when he had scored 19, Cowdrey received a cracking blow on the bone just above the left wrist and had to retire hurt.

The score was then 72 and an X-ray revealed that the bone was broken and the wrist was straightaway put into plaster. At that time no one knew whether Cowdrey would be available to resume batting or not, being sufficiently optimistic not to look so far ahead. But in bad light Barrington was playing one of his best Test innings, showing unusual aggression (he hit Gibbs for two 6s in one over) and with Close took the score to 116 for 3 when the light became too bad

England *v.* West Indies, Second Test at
Lord's 1963. Colin Cowdrey's dramatic
entrance with his left wrist in plaster.

at 4.45 and play was abandoned for the day.

So England still needed 118 to win with 6 wickets in hand plus Cowdrey to keep one end up, if necessary. But Tuesday was dark and wet, and play could not start until 2.20 p.m. So now with Hall and Griffith averaging no more than 14 overs per hour, time suddenly became an important factor, and England's chances were not helped by a very different Barrington from that of the day before. He made only 5 runs in 55 minutes and at the end of the first hour only 16 had been scored, which left 100 needed for victory in a possible 125 minutes. Close and Parks took the score to 158 and at tea the score was 171 for 5 with 63 runs needed in 85 minutes – still perfectly possible, but we kept reminding ourselves that with Cowdrey injured it was really 171 for 6 and that at the rate Hall and Griffith were bowling the run rate needed was at least 3½ per over.

After tea Titmus and Trueman fell to successive balls from Hall, and with Allen as his partner Close began to charge down the pitch against the fast bowlers. He was trying to knock them off their length and although he scored some runs on the leg-side, it was too dangerous a tactic to last and he was caught down the leg-side by wicket-keeper Murray. Close had made 70 valuable runs and had batted with great courage, finishing up with his body a mass of bruises. And so with 19 minutes left England were 219 for 8 when Shackleton joined Allen to try and get the 15 runs needed for victory. They managed to sneak 7 of these before Hall paced out his long run back to the Pavilion to start the last over of the match. Six balls left. Eight runs needed. Allen and Shackleton were both *normally* good for 20 or so runs. I say normally because this occasion was far from that. They knew that at a pinch Cowdrey would come out to act as non-striker but (with a broken wrist) could hardly be expected to stand up to the thunderbolts of Hall.

The tension on the ground was unbearable. English supporters in the crowd were hushed; West Indians were shouting encouragement to their heroes – especially big Wes. The eyes and ears of Great Britain were also sharing in the scene through TV and radio. Hall must have had memories of that final over at Brisbane as he set out on his long run. No score off the first ball, 1 run to Shackleton off the second and another to Allen off the third. Frank Worrell, the captain was calming and encouraging his side just as he had done at Brisbane, 'Relax fellows, relax.' He, as ever, looked the most relaxed of all as he stood quietly at forward short leg. Six runs were needed and only 3 balls left, so Shackleton clearly had to do something. He pushed the ball in front of him on the leg side and called for a run. The ball went straight to Worrell who, true to his maxim, did not panic. He saw the thirty-eight-year-old Shackleton setting off for the bowler's end and made a quick decision. He wouldn't throw at the stumps – Wes Hall wasn't behind them anyway. He may or may not have remembered that he too was aged thirty-eight. Anyway, he backed himself to outsprint Shackleton and, turning with the ball, ran to the bowlers end, knocking off the bails a split second before Shackleton arrived breathless at the crease. So Shackleton was run out and Cowdrey had to come in to join Allen.

Six runs still wanted, 2 balls to go. So in theory any of four results was possible but I don't believe that Allen ever intended to go for the runs. Had he scored an odd number, Cowdrey would have had to face a ball as a left-hander holding the bat with the right hand only. Of course you may ask why Allen didn't try to hit a 6 off the last ball. But be honest. Would you have done so? At all events he played the last 2 balls from Hall with a dead bat and the match was a draw – one of the greatest since cricket began and proof that for a game to be great one side needn't necessarily win. I think that both teams were equally happy to settle for a draw and so too, I think, were the spectators. Both sides deserved to win, neither deserved to lose.

THE SECOND TEST MATCH
Played at Lord's, 20, 21, 22, 24 and 25 June
Match drawn

WEST INDIES

C C Hunte	c Close b Trueman	44	c Cowdrey b Shackleton .	7
E D A McMorris	lbw b Trueman	16	c Cowdrey b Trueman	8
G S Sobers	c Cowdrey b Allen	42	c Parks b Trueman	8
R B Kanhai	c Edrich b Trueman	73	c Cowdrey b Shackleton .	21
B F Butcher	c Barrington b Trueman .	14	lbw b Shackleton	133
J S Solomon	lbw b Shackleton	56	c Stewart b Allen	5
†F M M Worrell	b Trueman	0	c Stewart b Trueman	33
‡D L Murray	c Cowdrey b Trueman	20	c Parks b Trueman	2
W W Hall	not out	25	c Parks b Trueman	2
C C Griffith	c Cowdrey b Shackleton .	0	b Shackleton	1
L R Gibbs	c Stewart b Shackleton ...	0	not out	1
Extras	(b 10, lb 1)	11	(b 5, lb 2, nb 1)	8
Total		301		229

ENGLAND

M J Stewart	c Kanhai b Griffith	2	c Solomon b Hall	17
J H Edrich	c Murray b Griffith	0	c Murray b Hall	8
† E R Dexter	lbw b Sobers	70	b Gibbs	2
K F Barrington	c Sobers b Worrell	80	c Murray b Griffith	60
M C Cowdrey	b Gibbs	4	not out	19
D B Close	c Murray b Griffith	9	c Murray b Griffith	70
‡J M Parks	b Worrell	35	lbw b Griffith	17
F J Titmus	not out	52	c McMorris b Hall	11
F S Trueman	b Hall	10	c Murray b Hall	0
D A Allen	lbw b Griffith	2	not out	4
D Shackleton	b Griffith	8	run out	4
Extras	(b 8, lb 8, nb 9)	25	(b 5, lb 8, nb 3)	16
Total		297	(9 wkts)	228

62

ENGLAND	O	M	R	W		O	M	R	W	
Trueman	44	16	100	6	...	26	9	52	5	
Shackleton	50.2	22	93	3	...	34	14	72	4	
Dexter	20	6	41	0	...					
Close	9	3	21	0	...					
Allen	10	3	35	1	...	21	7	50	1	
Titmus					...	17	3	47	0	

BOWLING

WEST INDIES	O	M	R	W		O	M	R	W
Hall	18	2	65	1	...	50	9	93	4
Griffith	26	6	91	5	...	30	7	59	3
Sobers	18	4	45	1	...	4	1	4	0
Gibbs	27	9	59	1	...	17	7	56	1
Worrell	13	6	12	2	...				

FALL OF WICKETS

	WI 1st	E 1st	WI 2nd	E 2nd
1st	51	2	15	15
2nd	64	20	15	27
3rd	127	102	64	31
4th	145	115	84	130
5th	219	151	104	158
6th	219	206	214	203
7th	263	235	224	203
8th	297	271	226	219
9th	297	274	228	228
10th	301	297	229	

Umpires: J S Buller and W E Phillipson

† Captain   ‡ Wicket-keeper

WEST INDIES v. ENGLAND – GEORGETOWN, GUYANA, 1968

I felt I must include in this book my most agonizing draw, that is a match saved by England after a long-drawn-out struggle when all had seemed lost. An Australian writing a similar book would be sure to pick the Fourth Test v. West Indies at Adelaide, 1961, when their last pair, Mackay and Kline, held out for an hour and fifty minutes to draw the match. Two Tests immediately came to my mind. First the Lord's Test of 1953 when England needed 343 to win, lost 3 quick wickets for 12 and with nearly 5 hours left were 73 for 4 when Trevor Bailey joined Willie Watson for their famous backs-to-the-wall stand of 163 for the fifth wicket. This undoubtedly saved England and I well remember the nail-biting tension of that long, hot summer afternoon. But somehow there always seemed *some* hope that England would be able to draw. Unlike the fifth Test at Georgetown, Guyana on the MCC Tour of the West Indies in 1967/68. That Test was the climax of a hard, tough, and thrilling series, where England, under Colin Cowdrey, so nearly won the first Test and almost lost the second after a bottle-throwing and tear-gas riot. After a dull draw in the third Test England won the fourth after a sporting declaration from Gary Sobers. So you can imagine that when they came to play the last Test, one up in the series, they were determined not to be beaten whatever happened. And yet how near they came to disaster in a tremendous six-day battle.

West Indies won the toss on a slowish pitch and made 414, Kanhai and Sobers in a 250 partnership scored 150 and 152 respectively, and John Snow claimed 4 wickets. When England batted, Boycott made a typical century and with Cowdrey (59) added 172. But when Lock was joined by Pocock, England were 259 for 8 and it looked as if the series was going to slip from their grasp. Lock, however, hit magnificently and with Pocock defending stubbornly (he was nearly an hour and a half without scoring), they added 109 for the ninth wicket – an English record against West Indies. Lock finished with 89 – the highest score of his first-class career – and England's total of 371 meant that they were 43 runs behind.

Except for a brilliant 49 by opening batsman Nurse and another great but more subdued innings of 95 not out by Sobers, the West Indies' batsmen in their second innings couldn't cope with John Snow. In seven balls, after lunch on the fifth day, he dismissed Nurse, Lloyd, and Camacho, and then later came back just before the close to clean-bowl King, Hall, and Gibbs. So Sobers ran out of partners and failed by 5 to score two 100s in the match. West Indies were all out for 264 and England on the last day needed 308 runs to win. Boycott and Edrich got them off to a good start by quickly scoring 30 off the fast bowlers. But then on came Gibbs and Sobers to bowl spin and England collapsed in dramatic fashion, Gibbs taking 4 wickets for 4 runs in 4 overs. Sobers trapped Edrich with his googly, then Boycott, Graveney, Barrington, and d'Oliveira all fell to Gibbs and England were 41 for 5 with just under 4 hours left.

Cowdrey was joined by Knott and although these two had batted superbly through the tour, I think every Englishman present at this moment saw only one result – a West Indies' victory and, with it, all Cowdrey's hopes and endeavours crashing to the ground. But some-how he and Knott stayed there against the wiles of Gibbs and Sobers who bowled over 70 overs between them in the innings. In an attempt to flurry the batsmen they got through their overs at a breathless pace, sacrificing somewhat their accuracy and direction in the process. Both batsmen used their pads more than one normally likes to see, but I must admit that at that stage I was prepared for them to do anything to survive, so long as it was legal! However, with 70 minutes still to go Cowdrey was lbw to Gibbs for 82. By a mixture of hitting the bad balls for 4 and keeping out the good balls they had added 127. But 70 minutes was a long time for tail-enders to last against the class spin of Gibbs and Sobers. Snow, who seemed to play *every* ball with his pads lasted 35 minutes before he, like Cowdrey, eventually misjudged the line and was lbw for a sterling 1.

Lock, somewhat desperate, lasted only 8 minutes and Pocock for 10, being unluckily given out 'caught' first bounce. All this time, Knott was defending sternly but hitting anything loose and wide of the stumps for 4 – especially with his favourite cut. Pocock was out amidst scenes of unbelievable excitement and shouting from the now frenzied crowd. The last man in, Jeff Jones, had one ball from

Gibbs to play and seemed to be in a complete daze. After all, his career batting average in first-class cricket was at that stage 4.09, so you can hardly blame him! Furthermore, he had been sitting watching this tense struggle all day and at close of play the night before could hardly have expected to be called on to play such a vital role! Anyway, with our hearts in our mouths we watched him lunge out with his pads at Gibbs and survive that one ball. Then Knott played an immaculate maiden over from Sobers. There was just time for one over and the result of the series depended on Jeff Jones.

The shouts from the crowd were deafening and it was impossible to give a fluent and coherent commentary. But somehow – and don't ask me how many times he hit the ball with his bat – Jeff Jones played out that last over, surrounded by the whole of the West Indies side. He might have let the ball hit his bat once but I mustn't exaggerate! But there he was 'not out' at the close of play, and gallant little Alan Knott had batted for nearly 4½ hours for 73 not out, which remarkably contained no fewer than 15 fours, so sure was his defence and so expert his dispatch of any bad ball. It is an innings he will never forget and certainly I don't want to go through such prolonged agony ever again.

FIFTH TEST MATCH
Played at Georgetown, 28, 29, 30, March, 1, 2 and 3 April
Match drawn

WEST INDIES

Batsman	Dismissal 1		Dismissal 2	
S M Nurse	c Knott b Snow	17	lbw b Snow	49
G S Camacho	c and b Jones	14	c Graveney b Snow	26
R B Kanhai	c Edrich b Pocock	150	c Edrich b Jones	22
B F Butcher	run out	18	c Lock b Pocock	18
†G S Sobers	c Cowdrey b Barrington	152	not out	95
C H Lloyd	b Lock	31	c Knott b Snow	1
D A J Holford	lbw b Snow	1	b Lock	3
‡D L Murray	c Knott b Lock	8	c Boycott b Pocock	16
L A King	b Snow	8	b Snow	20
W W Hall	not out	5	b Snow	7
L R Gibbs	b Snow	1	b Snow	0
Extras	(lb 3, w 2, nb 4)	9	(b 1, lb 2, w 1, nb 3)	7
Total		414		264

ENGLAND

Batsman	Dismissal 1		Dismissal 2	
G Boycott	c Murray b Hall	116	b Gibbs	30
J H Edrich	c Murray b Sobers	0	c Gibbs b Sobers	6
† M C Cowdrey	lbw b Sobers	59	lbw b Gibbs	82
T W Graveney	c Murray b Hall	27	c Murray b Gibbs	0
K F Barrington	c Kanhai b Sobers	4	c Lloyd b Gibbs	0
B L d'Oliveira	c Nurse b Holford	27	c and b Gibbs	2
‡ A P E Knott	lbw b Holford	7	not out	73
J A Snow	b Gibbs	0	lbw b Sobers	1
G A R Lock	b King	89	c King b Sobers	2
P I Pocock	c and b King	13	c Lloyd b Gibbs	0
I J Jones	not out	0	not out	0
Extras	(b 12, lb 14, nb 3)	29	(b 9, w 1)	10
Total		371	(9 wkts)	206

ENGLAND	O	M	R	W	O	M	R	W		WI 1st	E 1st	WI 2nd	E 2nd
Jones	31	5	114	1	17	1	81	1					
Snow	27.4	2	82	4	15.2	0	60	6	1st	29	13	78	33
d'Oliveira	8	1	27	0	8	0	28	0	2nd	35	185	84	37
Pocock	38	11	78	1	17	1	66	2	3rd	72	185	86	37
Barrington	18	4	43	1					4th	322	194	133	39
Lock	28	7	61	2	9	1	22	1	5th	385	240	171	41
WEST INDIES									6th	387	252	201	168
Sobers	37	15	72	3	31	16	53	3	7th	399	257	216	198
Hall	19	3	71	2	13	6	26	0	8th	400	259	252	200
King	38.2	11	79	2	9	1	11	0	9th	412	368	264	206
Holford	31	10	54	2	17	9	37	0	10th	414	371	264	
Gibbs	33	9	59	1	40	20	60	6					
Butcher	5	3	7	0	10	7	9	0					

Umpires: C Jordan and C Kippins

† Captain ‡ Wicket-keeper

ENGLAND v. AUSTRALIA – THE OVAL, 1968

My next choice is another Test which England won, thanks largely to the efforts of a volunteer ground staff who made it possible for play to be restarted on the last day when it appeared that a cloudburst had robbed England of a well-deserved victory. This was the fifth Test against Australia at the Oval in 1968. After losing the first Test, England were robbed of victory by bad weather in at least two of the following three, so that they had to win at the Oval to level the series. Cowdrey won the toss and England made 494 thanks to Edrich (164) and d'Oliveira, who made 158. D'Oliveira had been recalled to the England side at the last moment and until this fine attacking innings he had not been on many people's list for the forthcoming MCC tour of South Africa. The subsequent row which led to the cancellation of the tour is now cricket history.

Lawry was top scorer for Australia in their first innings with 135, but they were all out for 324 – 170 behind, due to some fine fast bowling by Snow and Brown who each took 3 wickets. But time was slipping away for England – it was already after lunch on the fourth day – and if they wanted to have a chance of winning they had to score runs quickly. This they did being all out for 181 in 3 hours – all the main batsmen flinging their bats at the ball. Australia therefore needed 352 to win in 6½ hours. That evening they lost both Lawry and Redpath. On the fifth morning the sun was still shining, as it had done throughout the match but there were ominous dark clouds gathering around the Oval. Underwood got Chappell and Walters, and Snow caught Sheahan off Illingworth, Inverarity being the only Australian batsman to show any real confidence. He and Jarman were together at lunch when Australia's score stood at 86 for 5.

With 3½ hours left, it looked odds on an England victory. But

A unique picture showing the entire
England team within a few yards of the
bat appealing for lbw against Inverarity.

during the lunch interval there was a colossal cloudburst. Within half an hour the whole ground was a lake and though the hot sun reappeared at 2.15 p.m. no one seriously thought there would be any more play in the match. No one, that is, except Colin Cowdrey and the groundsman Ted Warne. Cowdrey *paddled* out to inspect the damage and miraculously the big lake changed slowly into a number of mini-lakes as the water began draining away. Then Ted Warne and his ground staff, supported by a large number of volunteers from the crowd, got to work with blankets, mops, squeegees, and brooms. Incredible to relate, the umpires decided play could restart at 4.45 p.m., which meant that Australia had to survive for 75 minutes or England take their last 5 wickets in that time. Inverarity and Jarman defended stoutly for 38 minutes. The pitch was dead and Cowdrey switched his bowlers from end to end and crowded the batsmen with close fielders – all to no avail.

Then came the breakthrough which England needed. Cowdrey brought on d'Oliveira and in his second over he got a ball to hit Jarman's off-stump as he stretched forward and Australia were 110 for 6 with 35 minutes to go. For the next half an hour we were to watch some of the most gripping cricket which I personally have ever seen. Underwood at once came on in place of d'Oliveira, the fielders crowded even closer round the bat and the pitch which had had hot sun on it for nearly 3 hours began to come to life. Underwood got lift and turn, and batting, though not impossible, must have been a nightmare. Mallett and McKenzie were well caught by Brown at forward short leg in Underwood's first over of his new spell – 110 for 7, 110 for 8, and about 25 minutes left. In came Gleeson smiling cheerfully as usual, even in this crisis for his country. He actually shook hands with some of the close fielders as he took up his stance at the wicket! He lasted gallantly for nearly a quarter of an hour before being bowled by Underwood.

The score was 120 for 9 as Connolly strode out to join Inverarity with 10 minutes left. Inverarity had been in for 4 hours but only 6 minutes before time his concentration lapsed for once and he played no stroke at a ball from Underwood which didn't turn as much as he expected and struck him on the pad. There was a shout from everyone in the England side – the *farthest* fielder only 10 yards from the batsman. Without hesitation up went umpire Charlie Elliott's right arm and Inverarity was out for 56 and Australia for 125. England had won on the post by 226 runs. It will look an easy enough victory in the record books but an unsuspecting reader will never know how close it was. England had a lot for which to thank Underwood as he finished with figures of 7 for 50. But there is no doubt that their greatest debt was to the anonymous band of voluntary 'driers-up' who helped Ted Warne and his men to make a playable cricket ground out of a lake.

THE FIFTH TEST MATCH
Played at The Oval, 22, 23, 24, 26 and 27 August
England won by 226 runs

ENGLAND

J H Edrich	b Chappell	164	c Lawry b Mallett	17
C Milburn	b Connolly	8	c Lawry b Connolly	18
E R Dexter	b Gleeson	21	b Connolly	28
† M C Cowdrey	lbw b Mallett	16	b Mallett	35
T W Graveney	c Redpath b McKenzie	63	run out	12
B L d'Oliveira	c Inverarity b Mallett	158	c Gleeson b Connolly	9
‡A P E Knott	c Jarman b Mallett	28	run out	34
R Illingworth	lbw b Connolly	8	b Gleeson	10
J A Snow	run out	4	c Sheahan b Gleeson	13
D L Underwood	not out	9	not out	1
D J Brown	c Sheahan b Gleeson	2	b Connolly	1
Extras	(b 1, lb 11, w 1)	13	(lb 3)	3
Total		494		181

AUSTRALIA

† W M Lawry	c Knott b Snow	135	c Milburn b Brown	4
R J Inverarity	c Milburn b Snow	1	lbw b Underwood	56
I R Redpath	c Cowdrey b Snow	67	lbw b Underwood	8
I M Chappell	c Knott b Brown	10	lbw b Underwood	2
K D Walters	c Knott b Brown	5	c Knott b Underwood	1
A P Sheahan	b Illingworth	14	c Snow b Illingworth	24
‡ B N Jarman	st Knott b Illingworth	0	b d'Oliveira	21
G D McKenzie	b Brown	12	c Brown b Underwood	0
A A Mallett	not out	43	c Brown b Underwood	0
J W Gleeson	c Dexter b Underwood	19	b Underwood	5
A N Connolly	b Underwood	3	not out	0
Extras	(b 4, lb 7, nb 4)	15	(lb 4)	4
Total		324		125

BOWLING

AUSTRALIA	O	M	R	W	O	M	R	W
McKenzie	40	8	87	1	4	0	14	0
Connolly	57	12	127	2	22.4	2	65	4
Walters	6	2	17	0				
Gleeson	41.2	8	109	2	7	2	22	2
Mallett	36	11	87	3	25	4	77	2
Chappell	21	5	54	1				
ENGLAND								
Snow	35	12	67	3	11	5	22	0
Brown	22	5	63	3	8	3	19	1
Illingworth	48	15	87	2	28	18	29	1
Underwood	54.3	21	89	2	31.3	19	50	7
d'Oliveira	4	2	3	0	5	4	1	1

FALL OF WICKETS

	E	A	E	A
	1st	1st	2nd	2nd
1st	28	7	23	4
2nd	84	136	53	13
3rd	113	151	67	19
4th	238	161	90	29
5th	359	185	114	65
6th	421	188	˄26	110
7th	458	237	149	110
8th	468	269	179	110
9th	489	302	179	120
10th	494	324	181	125

Umpires: C S Elliott and A E Fagg

† Captain   ‡ Wicket-keeper

AUSTRALIA *v*. ENGLAND – SYDNEY, 1971

Commentating on winning the Ashes at the Oval in 1953 is a moment I shall never forget but one which I was lucky enough to be able to repeat when England regained the Ashes in the seventh Test at Sydney in February 1971. Once again – this time on radio – I was able to describe the final ball which brought the Ashes back to England, so I must include this final Test also in my selection. Even without that special quality which the Ashes gives to Test matches this was one of the most tense and closely fought Tests I have ever seen and like all really great games the fortunes of the two sides changed almost hourly throughout the five days.

To the relief of the England camp, Australia dropped Lawry and failed to select McKenzie. Had they played I feel sure the result would have been different. This is not a criticism of their new captain, Ian Chappell, who did a very good job and, on winning the toss, put England in to bat. England were without Boycott who had broken his arm, and on a lively pitch in a humid atmosphere had only scored 11 for 1 wicket at the end of the first hour. Luckhurst, for once, failed. Had McKenzie been bowling he must have taken some wickets. As it was, the inexperienced opening pair of Lillee

England captain, Ray Illingworth, is chaired off the field after England had regained the Ashes after twelve years.

and Dell bowled too short and were very wild in their direction. Even so, England struggled for most of the day. Edrich made 30 and Fletcher 33, but with d'Oliveira out for 1 they were 69 for 4 when Illingworth came to the wicket to play yet another of his rescue-act innings. Hampshire went for 10, but Knott lasted over an hour for a useful 27. By this time the two spinners Jenner and O'Keeffe were bowling really well. The pitch was taking spin and the innings closed for 184 with Illingworth eighth man out, bowled by Jenner's googly for the top score of 42. Jenner and O'Keeffe each took 3 wickets, and Chappell's gamble had come off in spite of the poor support from his fast bowlers. But Illingworth was luckier with his. Both Snow and Lever took a wicket in the half-hour left for play, and at the close Australia were 13 for 2 with both Eastwood and Stackpole out.

There was a hard tussle the next morning and in the 2 hours before lunch Australia added 71 and lost the wickets of nightwatchman Marsh and their captain, Ian Chappell. But after lunch Walters and Redpath added 63 in the first hour. Walters led a charmed life, being missed at slip off Underwood and at deep third man by Underwood off Willis. It also looked as if Knott had stumped him when he took a ball in front of the stumps off a mishit from Walters who was out of his crease. But it was great cricket to watch and a fascinating battle between the footwork of Redpath and Walters and the flight and change of pace of Underwood. He got them both in the end, Walters going yards down the pitch only to be stumped and Redpath giving a catch to the bowler when he had made 59. At tea the score was 165 for 6 representing a considerable drop in the scoring rate – only 18 runs coming in the second hour. O'Keeffe was soon out after tea, and with Greg Chappell and Jenner together the new ball was taken. Then followed the famous 'walk off' incident. I was broadcasting at the time so most of what happened is clear in my mind. For the rest I have checked and double-checked what happened out in the middle. I have set out the facts below so that you can judge for yourself and make up your own mind what you would have done had you been the captain in Illingworth's place – always remembering that you had a chance to sit back and think whereas he had to act on the spur of the moment.

The first two overs with the new ball were bowled by Snow and Lever with no suspicion of a bouncer. With the seventh ball of the third over, Snow, however, did bowl a bouncer at Jenner who ducked into it, was hit on the back of the head, collapsed, and had to be carried off. The crowd naturally enough booed and shouted, roaring their disapproval of Snow. While the new batsman Lillee was on his way out to the wicket, Lou Rowan, the umpire at Snow's end, told Snow that he should not have bowled a bouncer at a low-order batsman like Jenner. Snow became incensed at this and asked Rowan in not too polite a way whose side he thought he was on. Umpire Rowan then seemed to lose his temper and in what appeared to be an emotional decision, promptly warned Snow under Law 46 Note 4(IV) for persistent bowling of short-pitched balls. Then it was Illingworth's turn to protest at what he considered a wrong interpretation of the law. How could one bouncer come under the heading of persistent? Unfortunately, in the heat of the moment, Illingworth also became annoyed and was seen by thousands on the ground and tens of thousands on television to wag his finger at Lou Rowan. What in fact he was trying to indicate was that Snow had only bowled 'one' bouncer. He was not trying to admonish the umpire. Amid a storm of booing – I've seldom heard such a noise on a cricket ground – Snow completed his over by bowling one ball at Lillee. He then turned to go off to his position at long leg. When he had got halfway there some beer cans were thrown in his direction from the small Paddington Hill to the left of the Noble Stand. Snow turned back and returned to the square where Illingworth told the umpires that he would not go on playing until the field was cleared of the cans. The team sat down while this was being done by the ground staff. After a few minutes the ground was clear and Snow set off again for long leg.

I remember saying on the air at the time that I thought the whole incident was going to end happily as members in the Noble Stand and people on the hill started to applaud Snow and a man stretched out over the railings to shake hands with Snow. Snow went up and shook hands but a tough-looking spectator who had obviously 'had a few' then grabbed hold of Snow's shirt and started to shake him. This was the signal for more cans and bottles to come hurtling on to the field, narrowly missing Snow. Willis ran up and shouted something to the crowd. Then Illingworth came up, saw the bottles flying and promptly signalled to his team to leave the field. The two batsmen and two umpires stayed on the square. Then the two umpires made their way to the pavilion – the first time they had left the square since the trouble started. Rowan made it plain to Illingworth that if he did not continue he would forfeit the match and an announcement was made that play would be resumed as soon as the ground had been cleared, not only of the cans and bottles but also a number of spectators who had clambered over the fence. This, in fact, took only 10 minutes and Illingworth led his men back 13 minutes after leading them off. In the remaining 40 minutes, the

England side somewhat naturally seemed to have lost their zest, and Chappell and Lillee added 45 runs so that Australia finished the day at 235 for 7 – a lead of 51.

That was the incident as I saw it, though it is true to say that opinions differ about what exactly did happen. I said at the time, and I still believe, that Illingworth was right to lead the side off. Not only was it becoming dangerous with bottles flying around, but this action so stunned the crowd that the throwing stopped immediately and play was very soon restarted. In other similar circumstances in the West Indies, the fielding side had stayed on the field and play had to be abandoned for the day. There was, of course, no excuse for Illingworth to argue in such a demonstrative manner with the umpire. He has since publicly said he was sorry he acted as he did and also concedes that he should have gone back to the square and warned the umpires that he was taking his team off. But he had to make a quick decision and it is surprising that neither umpire left the square at any time to go to deal with the incident at the trouble spot. Illingworth and Snow have also been criticized for Snow's return to long leg after the first lot of cans had been thrown at him. There are two views about this. As captain, you either take the peaceful way out and give way to force and threats or you stick to your right to place your fieldsmen where you like. And finally, Snow was criticized for going up to the fence and accepting the proffered handshake. Who can say what the reaction would have been if he hadn't? I apologize for dealing at such length with this unhappy incident and now you must judge for yourselves. Meanwhile, let's get back to the cricket which continued on the Sunday morning.

Lillee was out to the first ball of the day, caught by Knott off Willis, who 2 overs later bowled Greg Chappell behind his legs for a fighting 65. Jenner came in at the fall of the first wicket, showing no after-effects from his injury and he made a bright 30 before being last man out, bowled by Lever. Australia were all out for 264, giving them a lead of 80 runs, and in the 70 minutes before lunch, Luckhurst and Edrich put on 60 with the former playing some brilliant strokes. He was out soon after lunch for 59, Fletcher made 20 and by tea England had made very slow progress to reach a score of 130 for 2. Two more wickets – Edrich 57 and Hampshire 24, fell before the close when England were 228 for 4 – leading by 149 runs. They owed a lot to d'Oliveira and Illingworth who stayed together for the last hour and a half and added 64. However, next morning, Illingworth was soon lbw to Lillee for 29 and d'Oliveira caught in the slips off Lillee for 47. Only 34 runs came in the first hour – Knott making 15 of them. England had still not anywhere near enough runs.

However, Lever and Snow each hit out scoring 17 and 20 respectively, but when England were all out for 302, they had lost their last 6 wickets for only 73 runs – O'Keeffe with 3 wickets again looking the most dangerous Australian bowler. Australia needed 223 runs to win in 15½ hours (a sixth day could be used if necessary) – an easy enough task most people thought, even though Australia had not got the steadying influence of Lawry.

They made a bad start – Snow yorking Eastwood for 0 in the first over. But then came tragedy for England. Stackpole hit a short ball from Lever high in the direction of long leg. Snow ran in to make the catch but came too far. He turned to try to make the catch before the ball went over the boundary but somehow overbalanced and caught the little finger of his bowling hand in the fence and broke it. He went off in great pain with the bone protruding through the skin – a horrid sight. Umpire Lou Rowan signalled 6 although in fact the ball had hit the fence and had not gone full pitch over it. This was the testing time for England, already without their best batsman and now cruelly robbed of their best bowler.

But Illingworth outwardly remained as calm as usual, though what he was thinking one can well imagine. Were the Ashes going to slip away from him after all? But the team rallied round him magnificently, Lever soon got Ian Chappell for 6, Illingworth himself had Redpath caught for 14 and bowled Stackpole, sweeping, for yet another fine innings of 67. At the close of play, Australia were 123 for 5 with Chappell and Marsh the not-out batsmen. The other wicket to fall had been Walters who again showed his dislike of fast bowling. This time he played an incredible shot – an upper cut – off a short ball from Willis and was caught chest high on the boundary in front of the pavilion at third man! So with two days to go if necessary, Australia needed exactly 100 to win and it was really anybody's match, with Australians tending to think England would win, and vice versa.

Once again the England side backed up Illingworth superbly and he himself, in his longest bowling spell of the series, bowled magnificently. Underwood bowled Marsh, hitting desperately across the line, for 16, and the score was 131 for 6. Knott stumped Chappell off Illingworth – 142 for 7, but O'Keeffe put up a stout defence and had been in for nearly an hour when Illingworth brought on d'Oliveira who virtually finished off the match. He dismissed O'Keeffe and Lillee in successive balls and though Dell saved the hat-trick and hung on with Jenner for twelve tense minutes, at 12.37 it was all over and the Ashes were ours. Jenner snicked a ball on to his pads and it flew to Fletcher at silly point who made the catch and the England team made straight for their captain, Illingworth, and carried him off the field.

England had won by 62 runs and what a wonderful cricket match it had been. It was of course a personal triumph for Illingworth who led his team magnificently in the field, encouraging and sustaining their morale. In addition he had borne the brunt of the bowling after Snow went off and his second innings figures of 20–7–39–3 did much to win the match. But it was also essentially a team effort and I shall always be glad that I was there to share their happiness in their hour of triumph on bringing back the Ashes to England after twelve years.

THE SEVENTH TEST MATCH
Played at Sydney, 12, 13, 14, 16 and 17 February
England won by 62 runs

ENGLAND

J H Edrich	c G Chappell b Dell	30	c I Chappell b O'Keeffe	57
B W Luckhurst	c Redpath b Walters	0	c Lillee b O'Keeffe	59
K W R Fletcher	c Stackpole b O'Keeffe	33	c Stackpole b Eastwood	20
J H Hampshire	c Marsh b Lillee	10	c I Chappell b O'Keeffe	24
B L d'Oliveira	b Dell	1	c I Chappell b Lillee	47
† R Illingworth	b Jenner	42	lbw b Lillee	29
‡A P E Knott	c Stackpole b O'Keeffe	27	b Dell	15
J A Snow	b Jenner	7	c Stackpole b Dell	20
P Lever	c Jenner b O'Keeffe	4	c Redpath b Jenner	17
D L Underwood	not out	8	c Marsh b Dell	0
R G D Willis	b Jenner	11	not out	2
Extras	(b 4, lb 4, w 1, nb 2)	11	(b 3, lb 3, nb 6)	12
Total		184		302

AUSTRALIA

K H Eastwood	c Knott b Lever	5	b Snow	0
K R Stackpole	b Snow	6	b Illingworth	67
‡R W Marsh	c Willis b Lever	4	b Underwood	16
†I M Chappell	b Willis	25	c Knott b Lever	6
I R Redpath	c and b Underwood	59	c Hampshire b Illingworth	14
K D Walters	st Knott b Underwood	42	c d'Oliveira b Willis	1
G S Chappell	b Willis	65	st Knott b Illingworth	30
K J O'Keeffe	c Knott b Illingworth	3	c sub. b d'Oliveira	12
T J Jenner	b Lever	30	c Fletcher b Underwood	4
D K Lillee	c Knott b Willis	6	c Hampshire b d'Oliveira	0
A R Dell	not out	3	not out	3
Extras	(lb 5, w 1, nb 10)	16	(b 2, nb 5)	7
Total		264		160

BOWLING

AUSTRALIA	O	M	R	W	O	M	R	W
Lillee	13	5	32	1	14	0	43	2
Dell	16	8	32	2	26.7	3	65	3
Walters	4	0	10	1	5	0	18	0
G Chappell	3	0	9	0				
Jenner	16	3	42	3	21	5	39	1
O'Keeffe	24	8	48	3	26	8	96	3
Eastwood					5	0	21	1
Stackpole					3	1	8	0

FALL OF WICKETS

	E 1st	A 1st	E 2nd	A 2nd
1st	5	11	94	0
2nd	60	13	130	22
3rd	68	32	158	71
4th	69	66	165	82
5th	98	147	234	96
6th	145	162	251	131
7th	156	178	276	142

ENGLAND														
					...					8th	165	235	298	154
Snow	18	2	68	1	...	2	1	7	1	9th	165	239	299	154
Lever	14.6	3	43	3	...	12	2	23	1	10th	184	264	302	160
d'Oliveira	12	3	24	0	...	5	1	15	2					
Willis	12	1	58	3	...	9	1	32	1					
Underwood	16	3	39	2	...	13.6	5	28	2					
Illingworth	11	3	16	1	...	20	7	39	3					
Fletcher					...	1	0	9	0					

Umpires: T F Brooks and L P Rowan

† Captain   ‡ Wicket-keeper

ENGLAND v. AUSTRALIA – HEADINGLEY, 1981

My sixth and final choice must be this remarkable Test which England won by 18 runs. It is true to say that no Test match in my time has had a bigger effect on the cricketing public. There was drama before it even started. England, under the captaincy of Ian Botham, narrowly lost the first Test at Trent Bridge largely due to a spate of dropped catches. The second Test at Lord's was drawn with Botham making a 'pair' and promptly resigning the captaincy.

So the third Test at Headingley saw Mike Brearley return as captain of England. Everyone was wondering how Botham would react to playing under someone else and whether Brearley could help him recapture the all-round form which he so sadly seemed to have lost.

So far as Brearley was concerned it was not a very encouraging start. He lost the toss and Australia batted first making 401 for 9 declared. But Botham salvaged *his* reputation by taking 6 for 95. Brearley's misfortunes continued. England were all out for 174 of which he made 10, and when England followed on he was again out for a small score – 14. England were soon 135–7 with Botham still there firing on all cylinders, but with England still 92 runs behind with just three wickets to fall.

From then on the fairy tale of this amazing Test changed from fantasy to sensational fact. Graham Dilley joined Botham. They had a short conference and are said to have decided that the only solution to such a desperate situation was to give it 'a bit of humpty'. In other words they were going to attack and try to dominate the Australian bowlers. And how well they succeeded. Dilley is a left hander, very strong and by nature a clean hitter. At the other end was Botham now in a ferocious mood and playing some highly unorthodox but brilliantly effective strokes. Together for the 8th wicket they added 117 in 80 minutes – only 7 short of an English record against Australia. The bowling was in disarray, and when Dilley was finally bowled by Alderman for 56 – at that time his highest first-class score – Botham was joined by Chris Old. These two added another 67 runs and at close of play England were 351 for 9, Willis somehow lasting out for 45 minutes. They now had the slender lead of 124 runs but what a dramatic change from the position three hours earlier. Botham was 149 not out – a fantastic innings. His hundred included 1 six and 19 fours – 82 runs in boundaries. That speaks for itself and confirmed for many of us that he is the finest hitter of a cricket ball that we have ever seen.

But back to the drama of the final day. Botham managed to hit one more four before Willis was out for one of the best two's he has ever scored! Australia needed only 130 runs to win, so perhaps it was not so surprising that Lillee and Marsh accepted Ladbroke's generous odds of 500–1 against an England victory!

England's batting recovery had been sensational enough. But what was to follow was even more unbelievable. Brearley started off with Botham bowling downhill from the Kirkstall Lane end and with Willis trundling *up*hill and *up* wind from the football stand end. This worked, because Botham soon got Wood caught by Taylor behind the wicket and Australia were 13–1. But then nothing happened for over an hour. Dilley was tried, Old replaced Botham, and Australia progressed steadily to 56 for 1 only 74 runs needed for victory with 9 wickets in hand.

Brearley then switched Willis to the Kirkstall Lane end. It was like a magician waving his wand. Willis began to bowl faster than we had ever seen him. He produced prodigious bounce out of this fairly placid pitch. As a bowler he was transformed and accomplished the finest bowling performance of his career. It was fantastic cricket. The crowd began to roar, life in Great Britain came to a halt. Every TV set and radio in the country must have been tuned in to hear the Australian wickets tumbling at an extraordinary rate, 56 for 1 soon became 75 for 8, six of the wickets falling to Willis. There was a short desperate stand of 35 between Lillee and Bright which took the score up to 110, and Australia must have begun to think that they would just manage to snatch a victory, which by all reasonable expectations, should have been theirs the previous afternoon. But Willis was still inspired. He took the last two wickets to finish with his best ever analysis of 8 for 43 and England had won by 18 runs. It must certainly rank as the most astonishing turn around in any Test match. It was impossible to take it in at the time. It was all so incredible.

It was clearly Botham's and Willis's match and thanks to them Brearley had succeeded in creating a new spirit of enthusiasm throughout the country. Cricket became the main talking point whenever people met. Two more amazing performances by Botham (5 for 11 at Edgbaston, and 118 in 123 minutes including 6 sixes at

Old Trafford) enabled England to win the series 3–1 and so retain the Ashes.

Just one interesting footnote to Willis's tremendous bowling. I asked him later why he, the oldest and the fastest bowler in the side should have had to bowl uphill and upwind at the start of the Australian second innings. He told me that he had wondered the same thing and had told Brearley that he was getting too old for that sort of thing, and could he have a go *down* wind. He also asked Brearley why he had put him on at that end anyway. 'To make you angry!' was Brearley's reply. What captaincy! What insight into Willis's character! And how it worked!

THE THIRD TEST MATCH
Played at Headingley, 16, 17, 18, 20 and 21 July
England won by 18 runs

ENGLAND

G Boycott	b Lawson	12	lbw b Alderman	46
G A Gooch	lbw Alderman	2	c Alderman b Lillee	0
†J M Brearley	c Marsh b Alderman	10	c Alderman b Lillee	14
D I Gower	c Marsh b Lawson	24	c Border b Alderman	9
M W Gatting	lbw Lillee	15	lbw Alderman	1
P Willey	b Lawson	8	c Dyson b Lillee	33
I T Botham	c Marsh b Lillee	50	not out	149
‡R W Taylor	c Marsh b Lillee	5	c Bright b Alderman	1
R G D Willis	not out	1	c Border b Alderman	2
G R Dilley	c and b Lillee	13	b Alderman	56
C M Old	c Border b Alderman	0	b Lawson	29
Extras		34		16
Total		174		356

AUSTRALIA

J Dyson	b Dilley	102	c Taylor b Willis	34
G M Wood	lbw b Botham	34	c Taylor b Botham	10
T M Chappell	c Taylor b Willey	27	c Taylor b Willis	8
†K J Hughes	c and b Botham	99	c Botham b Willis	0
G N Yallop	c Taylor b Botham	58	c Gatting b Willis	0
A R Border	lbw b Botham	8	b Old	0
‡R W Marsh	b Botham	28	c Dilley b Willis	4
R J Bright	b Dilley	7	b Willis	19
D K Lillee	not out	3	c Gatting b Willis	17
G F Lawson	c Taylor b Botham	13	c Taylor b Willis	1
T M Alderman	not out	0	not out	0
Extras		32		18
Total (9 wkts declared)		401		111

BOWLING

AUSTRALIA	O	M	R	W	O	M	R	W
Lillee	18.5	7	49	4	25	6	94	3
Alderman	19	4	59	3	35.3	6	135	6
Lawson	13	3	32	3	23	4	96	1
Bright					4	0	15	0

FALL OF WICKETS

	E	A	E	A
	1st	1st	2nd	2nd
1st	12	55	0	13
2nd	40	149	18	56
3rd	42	196	37	58

ENGLAND

										4th	84	220	41	58
Willis	30	8	72	0	...	15.1	3	43	8	5th	87	332	105	65
Old	43	14	91	0	...	9	1	21	1	6th	112	354	133	68
Dilley	27	4	78	2	...	2	0	11	0	7th	148	357	135	74
Botham	39.2	11	95	6	...	7	3	14	1	8th	166	396	252	75
Willey	13	2	31	1	...	3	1	4	0	9th	167	401	319	110
Boycott	3	2	2	0	...					10th	174		356	111

Umpires: B J Meyer and D L Evans

† Captain   ‡ Wicket-keeper

My Forty-two Greats

WHY FORTY-TWO? Because at the time of writing I have been lucky enough to commentate for the BBC on Test cricket for the last forty years, 24 years on TV, 16 on Test Match Special. By the time this book is published I hope to have already commentated on at least one Test in 1986, making it forty-one years. And just for luck – and hoping! I have thrown in the following year, 1987.

I owe a debt of thanks to all these great cricketers not only for the enjoyment which they have given me, but because they have always been so friendly and helpful to me.

I have arranged my 'batting' order by putting one name against each year. Where possible I have made if fit in with something significant in the cricketer's career, e.g. 1947 Compton's Golden Summer, 1948 Bradman's Last Test or 1956 Laker's 19 wickets at Old Trafford. I am conscious that I have inevitably left out other great Test cricketers such as Dexter, Hanif Mohammad, Holding, Willis and so on.

I leave you to pick your first and second XIs from these forty-two names. Or even to select a team of those *not* included to beat them!

In the batting records an asterisk denotes a 'Not Out' innings and H.S. stands for Highest Score.

1946: Walter Hammond

Gloucestershire and England
Born: 19 July 1903
Died: 1 July 1965
Career: 1920–51

Captained England twenty times from 1938 to 1947. Was one of the truly great all-rounders of all time, famous for his classic cover drive and powerful strokes off the back foot – even in defence. His figures speak for themselves but give no indication of the power and authority which raised him head and shoulders above his contemporaries. There was an aura of majesty about the way he 'glided' to the wicket or moved about in the field. A superb fielder with a wonderful eye, he was one of the best slip fielders of all time, pouching even the most difficult catches in an insolent way which made them look easy. He was also a fine medium bowler with pace off the pitch and had he not been a batsman he might well have been as good as Maurice Tate.

BATTING

	Innings	Not Out	Highest Score	Runs	Average	Hundreds
Career	1,005	104	336*	50,551	56.10	167
Tests (85)	140	16	336*	7,249	58.45	22

BOWLING

	Balls	Runs	Wickets	Average	Best Bowling
Career	–	22,391	732	30.58	9 for 23
Tests	7,969	3,138	83	37.80	5 for 36

1947: Denis Compton

Middlesex and England
Born: 23 May 1918
Career: 1936–1964

The Cavalier of cricket with the dancing feet, unorthodox in attack, but strictly orthodox in defence. An entertainer who charmed with brilliant improvisation. In 1947 he made two records which he still holds – 18 hundreds and 3,816 runs in one season. He would dance yards down the pitch to the slow, and sometimes even to the fast bowlers. His favourite scoring strokes – the late chop, the cover drive anywhere from behind point to extra cover. the on-drive, the hook, and his own speciality – the sweep. This sometimes got him out, but it also scored him many hundreds of runs. Also a useful left-arm bowler with his 'chinaman' and googly, though his length was often sacrificed for spin. He was casual, handsome, forgetful of appointments, usually late, and often used other people's equipment because he had lost or forgotten his own. Must go down on record as being the worst judge of a run of any of the top-class batsmen. To answer his calls was like booking a ticket back to the pavilion. But it is cricketers like him who pull in the crowds, who for their entertainment prefer something different from their normal everyday life – and there was nothing normal about Compton!

BATTING

	Innings	Not Out	Highest Score	Runs	Average	Hundreds
Career	839	88	300	38,942	51.85	123
Tests (78)	131	15	278	5,807	50.06	17

BOWLING

	Balls	Runs	Wickets	Average	Best Bowling
Career	–	20,074	622	32.27	7 for 36
Tests	2,716	1,410	25	56.40	5 for 70

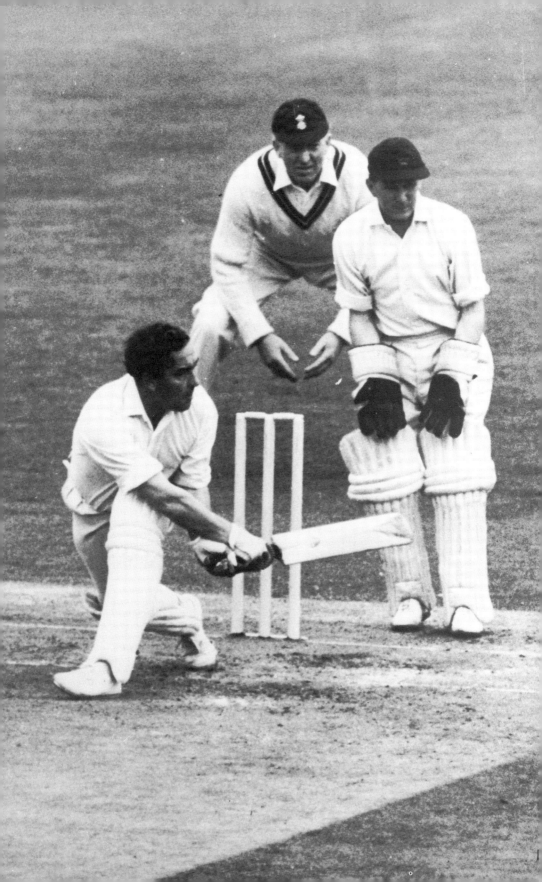

1948: Don Bradman

New South Wales, South Australia and Australia
Born: 27 August 1908. Knighted in 1948
Career: 1927/8–48/9

The greatest run-making machine ever seen in cricket. He had
beautiful footwork, a wonderful eye, tremendous powers of concentration, and all the strokes. Believed in attacking the bowler from
the very first ball and in staying on top throughout the longest
innings. A fine judge of a run who ran every one as fast as he could,
he enjoyed making big scores and never gave his wicket away. If he
had not been bowled second ball for 0 by Hollies in his last Test
innings at the Oval in 1948, he would have had a Test average of 100
or more. He always scored his runs at an amazing rate and at
Headingley in 1930 he actually made 309 not out on the first day of
the Test. A brilliant fielder anywhere away from the wicket, he was
voted by many as the best batsman of all time, though he was never
as skilful on a turning wicket as many English batsmen. On the type
of pitches he played on he seldom had need to be. He captained
Australia twenty-four times. Bradman was tough, unyielding, fair,
and as one might expect from a man with such a profound knowledge of cricket, also possessed great strategic sense.

BATTING

	Innings	Not Out	Highest Score	Runs	Average	Hundreds
Career	338	43	452*	28,067	95.14	117
Tests (52)	80	10	334	6,996	99.94	29

1949: Ray Lindwall

New South Wales, Queensland and Australia
Born: 3 October 1921
Career: 1941/2–61/2

One of the fastest bowlers of all time with a copy-book action and a wonderfully smooth run-up. He had complete command over length and direction and moved the ball very late either into or away from the batsman. With Keith Miller he formed a formidable, fearsome and ferocious opening attack for Australia. He was a fine fielder and a more than useful No. 8 or 9 batsman.

BOWLING

	Balls	Runs	Wickets	Average	Best Bowling
Career	–	16,956	794	21.35	7 for 20
Tests	13,650	5,251	228	23.03	7 for 38

BATTING

	Innings	Not Out	Highest Score	Runs	Average	Hundreds
Career	270	39	134*	5,042	21.82	5
Tests (61)	84	13	118	1,502	21.15	2

85

1950: Arthur Morris

New South Wales and Australia
Born: 19 January 1922
Career: 1940/1–63/4

A left-hander and one of the most stylish opening batsmen ever produced by Australia. Although an opener, thanks to his good footwork he played the spinners even better than he did the fast bowlers. He always liked to attack the bowling. A very friendly and pleasant personality.

BATTING

	Innings	Not Out	Highest Score	Runs	Average	Hundreds
Career	250	15	290	12,614	53.67	46
Tests (46)	79	3	206	3,533	46.48	12

1951: Keith Miller

Victoria New South Wales and Australia
Born: 28 November 1919
Career: 1937/8–59

A dynamic, handsome, debonair crowd-puller and a genuine all-rounder of the highest class. He enjoyed life, and his cricket matched his character. When in form, could drive with great power, but often nearly did the splits when stretching out to slow bowlers. Was a fearsome and devastating fast bowler, who could bowl six different balls in one over, including even a googly or beamer – all of them from a different length of run. For such a jovial character he gave the appearance of hating batsmen and showed them little mercy, though he was never slow to applaud them if they hooked his most terrifying bumper for 6. A deceptively casual slip fielder who seldom dropped a catch.

BATTING

	Innings	Not Out	Highest Score	Runs	Average	Hundreds
Career	326	36	281*	14,183	48.90	41
Tests	55	7	147	2,958	36.97	7

BOWLING

	Balls	Runs	Wickets	Average	Best Bowling
Career	–	11,087	497	22.30	7 for 12
Tests	10,461	3,906	170	22.97	7 for 60

1952: Alec Bedser

Surrey and England
Born: 4 July 1918
Career: 1939–60

Nicknamed 'big fella', this much loved character was one of the best medium-pace bowlers who ever played cricket. He had a perfect swivel bowling action and bowled an impeccable length and direction, making the ball fizz off the pitch like Maurice Tate had done before him. A master in-swinger, he later learned to bowl what was sometimes an unplayable leg-cutter. He liked his wicket-keepers to stand up close to the stumps to 'give him something to aim at'. As a batsman he was a solid tail-ender with a top Test score of 79. Elected Chairman of the England selectors in 1969, he retained that post until 1981.

		BOWLING			
	Balls	Runs	Wickets	Average	Best Bowling
Career	–	39,281	1,924	20.41	8 for 18
Tests (51)	15,918	5,876	236	24.89	7 for 44

1953: Clyde Walcott

Barbados, British Guiana and West Indies
Born: 17 January 1926
Career: 1941/2–63/4

One of the three 'W's' who dominated West Indian cricket in the 'fifties. A large man, 6 feet 2 inches tall, he hit the ball tremendously hard and there was never much competition to field in front of the wicket when he was on the attack. Being a good hooker and cutter he was particularly severe on anything pitched short. Kept wicket or fielded at slip and also bowled medium-paced swingers.

BATTING

	Innings	Not Out	Highest Score	Runs	Average	Hundreds
Career	238	29	314*	11,820	56.55	40
Tests (44)	74	7	220	3,798	56.68	15

BOWLING

	Balls	Runs	Wickets	Average	Best Bowling
Career	–	1,269	35	36.25	5 for 41
Tests	1,194	408	11	37.09	3 for 50

1954: Everton Weekes

Barbados and West Indies
Born: 26 February 1925
Career: 1944/5–63/4

The second of the three 'W's'. A magnificent stroke player who believed in attacking and at the same time turned out the runs like a sausage machine. Once scored five Test hundreds in succession, and was run out for 90 going for the sixth. A brilliant fielder anywhere.

BATTING

	Innings	Not Out	Highest Score	Runs	Average	Hundreds
Career	241	24	304*	12,010	55.34	36
Tests (48)	81	5	207	4,455	58.61	15

1955: Len Hutton

Yorkshire and England
Born: 23 June 1916. Knighted in 1956
Career: 1934–60

Until beaten by Gary Sobers in 1958, Hutton held the record Test score of 364 which he made against Australia at the Oval in 1938. He was the first professional to be appointed captain of England in England. Still holds the record of the most runs made in one month – 1,294 in June 1949. Had a wonderful technique allied with a phlegmatic temperament. He had to withstand a terrible battering from Lindwall and Miller at a time when England's batting depended largely upon his success. Although he injured his right arm in the war so that it was shorter than his left, he was a model for schoolboys to copy with an exquisite off-drive. He could be criticized for not using his feet to the slow bowlers, preferring to play them from the crease. His answer could be, 'Well, look at my record,' and one must admit that the method he used certainly seemed to suit him. Most definitely qualifies as one of the best opening batsmen of all time. As a captain he won back the Ashes for England and never lost a series against another country. A true Yorkshireman, he hated the enemy and played hard to win or at least to avoid defeat. Sometimes used tactics, which although within the laws, spoiled the game as a spectacle – e.g. deliberately engineering a slow over rate.

BATTING

	Innings	Not Out	Highest Score	Runs	Average	Hundreds
Career	814	91	364	40,140	55.51	129
Tests (79)	138	15	364	6,971	56.67	19

1956: Jim Laker

Surrey, Essex and England
Born: 9 February 1922; Died 23 April 1986
Career: 1946–64/5

Will always be remembered for the incredible feat of taking 19 wickets in the fourth Test against Australia at Old Trafford in 1956. It was so incredible that it must surely always remain a Test match record. His total, too, of 46 wickets during the series is another England *v*. Australia record likely to stand. Admittedly, at Old Trafford the pitch helped him but that other great spinner, Tony Lock, bowled 69 overs in the match compared with Laker's 68 and yet only managed to take one wicket. Like most classic bowlers, Laker had the perfect action with his arm so high that it used to brush his right ear. He had everything – flight, spin, accuracy, and direction. He perfected the away 'floater' so that unsuspecting batsmen played for the off-break that never was and were often caught in the slips or behind the stumps. He was no mean batsman either, with a Test highest of 63, and he was also a safe catcher in the gully.

	Balls	Runs	Wickets	Average	Best Bowling
BOWLING					
Career	–	35,791	1,944	18.41	10 for 53
Tests (46)	12,027	4,101	193	21.24	10 for 53

1957: Peter May

Surrey and England
Born: 31 December 1929
Career: 1948–63

Captained England forty-one times – more than any other Test captain. Stands very high up on the world list of top-class batsmen and had a wonderful defensive technique and fine attacking strokes, especially his classical on-drive. Hit a 100 in his first Test for England at the age of twenty-one and from then on, whenever he was playing, the other England batsmen, however good, seemed to bat in his shadow. Off the field he was quiet, shy, sensitive, but friendly. On it he was tough, played hard, and conceded nothing. Without quite being able to pinpoint the reason I place him in a class above all his contemporaries. He was appointed Chairman of the England selectors in 1982.

BATTING

	Innings	Not Out	Highest Score	Runs	Average	Hundreds
Career	618	77	285*	27,592	51.00	85
Tests (66)	106	9	285*	4,537	46.77	13

1958: Godfrey Evans

Kent and England
Born: 18 August 1920
Career: 1939–69

His 219 dismissals stood for 17 years as the wicket-keeping record in all Test cricket until Alan Knott broke it in 1976, followed by Rodney Marsh and Wasim Bari. Full of tireless energy, he was brilliant behind the stumps, and even at the end of the hottest day still walked as smartly between the wickets with his perky little steps as he had done at the end of the first over. He was essentially a showman, spectacular and acrobatic, hurling himself to make catches that no one else would even have attempted. Loved standing up to the faster bowlers and his taking of Alec Bedser's in-swinger outside the leg stump was a sight never to be forgotten. He was full of guts and kept the whole side and even his opponents cheerful! By running out to meet the returns he always did his best to make a mediocre throw look good. Had the occasional off-day and when he did it was a really bad one, e.g. the second innings of the 1948 Headingley Test when Australia made 404 to win in the fourth innings. But between 1946 and 1959 an England XI without Evans never looked the same and in fact, except for two Tests in South Africa in 1948–49, I cannot ever remember his being left out except for injury. As a batsman he always enjoyed himself, taking the cheekiest of singles, either hitting out at almost every ball (Lord's 1952 v. India – 98 before lunch), or defending as if his life depended on it (Adelaide, 1947, where he was 95 minutes at the wicket without scoring). He scored two Test hundreds. If there were more cricketers like Evans, the crowds would flock back to the grounds. Off the field he was a cheerful extrovert, always the life and soul of every party.

BATTING

	Innings	Not Out	Highest Score	Runs	Average	Hundreds
Career	753	52	144	14,882	21.22	7
Tests (91)	133	14	104	2,429	20.49	2

WICKET-KEEPING

Career	1,066 Dismissals (816 caught, 250 stumped)
Tests	219 Dismissals (173 caught, 46 stumped)

1959: Wally Grout

Queensland and Australia
Born: 30 March 1927
Died: 9 November 1968
Career: 1946/7–65/6

With his gruff nasal voice and tough aggressive exterior, Grout was typical of the old-style Australian cricketer. He always played to win, being a wonderful team man and a great help to his captain. Underneath it all he had a dry and often caustic sense of humour with a good command of language! He was aged thirty before he kept wicket for Australia but soon made up for his late start by getting 187 victims over a span of eight years. Remembered by most people for this remarkable catches off fast bowlers like Davidson and McKenzie. But to the connoisseur he was as quick as any stumper since the war and his work close to the stumps in 'reading' spinners like Benaud was a joy to watch. He could hit the ball hard on the leg-side and his top Test score was 74 against England at Melbourne in 1959. When he died of a heart attack in 1968 the Test scene seemed empty without him.

BATTING

	Innings	Not Out	Highest Score	Runs	Average	Hundreds
Career	253	24	119	5,168	22.56	3
Tests (51)	67	8	74	890	15.08	–

WICKET-KEEPING

Career	587 Dismissals (473 caught, 114 stumped)
Tests	187 Dismissals (163 caught, 24 stumped)

1960: Frank Worrell

Barbados, Jamaica and West Indies
Born: 1 August 1924. Knighted 1964
Died: 13 March 1967
Career: 1941/2–64

A fine all-round cricketer. Worrell will be best remembered for his magnificent captaincy of the West Indies between 1960–3 when he welded the different islanders into a real team representing West Indies. He was a born leader, dignified, calm, unflappable and firm. He was friendly and charming off the field, though on it he played hard to win. But he was always fair and his opponents respected him as much as did his own side. His early death at the age of forty-two was a sad loss for West Indian cricket. It was thanks to his soothing influence that the West Indies brought off that remarkable tie against Australia at Brisbane. As a right-hand batsman he was more orthodox but not as exciting as the other two 'W's'. He played straight with a copy-book off-drive and a superb late cut. As a left-arm bowler he varied from fast medium to slow – a forerunner of Sobers, although his slow bowling was orthodox left arm.

BATTING

	Innings	Not Out	Highest Score	Runs	Average	Hundreds
Career	326	49	308*	15,025	54.24	39
Tests (51)	87	9	261	3,860	49.48	9

BOWLING

	Balls	Runs	Wickets	Average	Best Bowling
Career	–	10,114	349	28.97	7 for 70
Tests	7,141	2,672	69	38.72	7 for 70

1961: Richie Benaud

New South Wales and Australia
Born: 6 October 1930
Career: 1948/9–67/8

Started his Test life as a useful leg-bowler and batsman who drove the ball fiercely. He finished his career as a genuine Test all-rounder (the first Test cricketer to score 2,000 runs and take 200 wickets). He was also one of the ablest and astutest captains Australia has ever had. He led them twenty-eight times in six series between 1958 and 1963, won five and drew the other one. A fine leader who encouraged his players to such an extent that he was even prepared to hug them if they took a good catch! A profound student of the game he was able to diagnose the strengths and weaknesses of the opposition. Was always prepared to play 'attacking' cricket if the other side played ball, but if they did not he could be as defensive as any captain. But, owing to his excellent sense of public relations, it was usually the other captain who got the blame!

He had a nice high action and, especially in Australia, South Africa, and the West Indies, got a lot of bounce out of the pitches. In England he was never such a threat to batsman except for his 6 for 70 bowling round the wicket into the rough at Old Trafford in 1961. He was not a big-spinner of the ball, but flighted it well. He bowled every variety, well disguised – googly, top spinner, and flipper, and could maintain an accurate length for long periods. He was a fine catcher in the gully and his batting grew in maturity until he became a complete batsman, but still with the drive as his strongest stroke.

BATTING

	Innings	Not Out	Highest Score	Runs	Average	Hundreds
Career	365	44	187	11,719	36.50	23
Tests (63)	97	7	122	2,201	24.45	3

BOWLING

	Balls	Runs	Wickets	Average	Best Bowling
Career	–	23,370	945	24.73	7 for 18
Tests	19,108	6,704	248	27.03	7 for 72

1962: Neil Harvey

Victoria, New South Wales and Australia
Born: 8 October 1928
Career: 1946/7–62/3

A small dapper left-hander with twinkling feet who matched up to the greatest batsmen Australia have ever had. He scored more Test runs than any Australian except Greg Chappell and Don Bradman. Essentially an attacking player he nevertheless had a very sound defence and was possibly the best bad wicket player that Australia ever produced. He had all the strokes but was a particularly fine cutter and ran beautifully between the wickets. A fast and brilliant fielder with a nice philosophy about cricket, namely that it was fun and a game to enjoy. When Benaud injured his shoulder in 1961, Harvey led Australia to victory in the second Test at Lord's.

BATTING

	Innings	Not Out	Highest Score	Runs	Average	Hundreds
Career	461	35	231*	21,699	50.93	67
Tests (79)	137	10	205	6,149	48.41	21

1963: Alan Davidson

New South Wales and Australia
Born: 14 June 1929
Career: 1949/50–62/3

Known as 'Davo', this broad-shouldered all-rounder both batted and bowled left-handed. His bowling was genuinely fast – over the wicket, with the ball going either across the batsman towards the slips, or swinging into him very late. This meant that every ball just outside the off stump had to be played in case it was the in-swinger. More often than not it was not and the result was a catch to the slips or wicket-keeper off the outside edge. With the new ball he was devastating and sometimes practically unplayable. He was also a fine forcing bat who really hit the ball and a superb fielder anywhere with a large pair of hands to help him make some astonishing catches. He had to be nursed and encouraged by his captain, and Benaud was especially adept at this. 'Davo' probably left the field more than any Test player, with some injury or other, which often seemed to the onlooker to be more imaginary than real. But when the crisis came, he was quite ready to leap off the massage table and renew battle with the enemy!

BATTING

	Innings	Not Out	Highest Score	Runs	Average	Hundreds
Career	246	39	129	6,804	32.86	9
Tests (44)	61	7	80	1,328	24.59	–

BOWLING

	Balls	Runs	Wickets	Average	Best Bowling
Career	–	14,048	672	20.90	7 for 31
Tests	11,587	3,819	186	20.53	7 for 93

1964: Freddie Trueman

Yorkshire and England
Born: 6 February 1931
Career: 1949–68

Fiery Fred was one of the greatest characters the game has ever known. A wonderful entertainer, who was loved by crowds all over the world and whose stock of swear-words must have rivalled the record number of 307 wickets which he took in Test matches. He played to the crowd, making ferocious gestures or expressions at the batsman, with his dark forelock hanging over his face. He was a tough, strong, belligerent Yorkshireman with a Rabelaisian wit and an occasional burst of temperament. In his prime he was genuinely fast and had a long curving run with a perfect action. He mostly moved the ball away from the batsmen. Like Keith Miller he could be merciless and hated batsmen, but was quite prepared to applaud a good stroke played off his bowling. He was a safe catcher close to the wicket and when 'resting' in the deep used to vary things by throwing in left-handed. Could defend stubbornly with a straight bat when the occasion demanded, but normally his object was to try and hit the ball out of the ground with the crookedest of bats. When he retired, cricket lost some of its colour. There are more stories told about him than any other cricketer – some true, some certainly apocryphal – many of them (because of the language difficulty!) being unprintable in a book like this. But one worth telling concerns the time when he came in to bat No. 10 for England in a Test against the West Indies in 1954, Jeff Stollmeyer was the opposing captain and crowded Freddie with four short legs, a silly mid-off point, gully, and two slips – all the fielders surrounding the stumps with Freddie glowering in the middle of them. 'If you bring any of these b---s in any closer I'll appeal against "flippin light"', said Freddie to Jeff. Fred has now become a very successful member of the BBC Radio 3 Test Match Special commentary team.

BOWLING

	Balls	Runs	Wickets	Average	Best Bowling
Career	–	42,154	2,304	18.29	8 for 28
Tests (67)	15,178	6,625	307	21.57	8 for 31

1965: Brian Statham

Lancashire and England
Born: 16 June 1930
Career: 1950–68

Known as 'George' to his friends and the perfect example of what a cricket professional should be. Quiet, modest, loyal, completely free from temperament, and a tremendous trier who would never give up – the captain's ideal bowler. Behind his slow Lancashire drawl there lay a fund of wit and cricket knowledge. Lanky, wiry, and apparently double-jointed he was also known as the 'greyhound'. He was deceptively fast with a smooth run-up and brought his arm over high. He was extremely accurate and bowled straight at the stumps, occasionally moving the ball off the pitch but seldom in the air. He formed a wonderful partnership with both Trueman and Tyson, and, typically, seemed to play second fiddle to both of them. Yet without him they would not have been half as effective. He was an excellent fielder with a splendid arm, and a good turn of speed. He batted left-handed, and could keep up his end in a crisis.

	BOWLING				
	Balls	Runs	Wickets	Average	Best Bowling
Career	–	36,995	2,260	16.36	8 for 34
Tests (70)	16,056	6,261	252	24.84	7 for 39

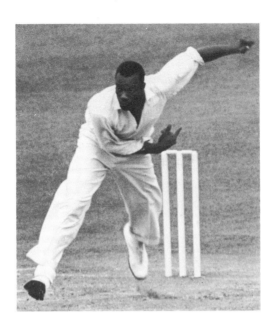

1966: Wes Hall

Barbados, Queensland, Trinidad and West Indies
Born: 12 September 1937
Career: 1955/6–70/1

The smiling and, at heart, gentle giant, with possibly the longest run-up of any fast bowler in history. Very fast and unpleasant to play, he relied more on his pace than any particular movement of the ball. His bumpers looked lethal though, luckily, they never were so in fact. Possessed remarkable stamina and could keep up his pace for long periods. A great mimic with a wide range of voices and a marvellous sense of humour he was a favourite with crowds wherever he played, especially when he batted. He rather fancied himself and played some copybook strokes which unfortunately didn't always connect with the ball. With Charlie Griffith he formed yet another fast-bowling partnership to follow in the steps of Gregory and McDonald. Larwood and Voce, Lindwall and Miller, Adcock and Heine, Trueman and Statham. Funny how they go in pairs! He was the bowler concerned in the dramatic last over on two celebrated occasions – the Brisbane tie in 1960 and the Lord's draw of 1963.

BOWLING

	Balls	Runs	Wickets	Average	Best Bowling
Career	–	14,273	546	26.14	7 for 51
Tests (48)	10,421	5,066	192	26.38	7 for 69

1967: Ken Barrington

Surrey and England
Born: 24 November 1930
Died: 14 March 1981
Career: 1953–68

A lovable character with a craggy face, large nose, engaging grin and a tendency to malapropisms. Started life with Surrey as a hard-hitting batsman and as such first played for England against South Africa in 1955. But he was dropped after two Tests and on his recall to Test cricket four years later had changed his style. He had worked out a defensive system which ensured survival, and with his new square-on stance became one of the most difficult of all Test batsmen to dislodge.

For the next nine years he was the Rock of Gibraltar and the sight of him walking determinedly to the wicket – chin stuck out – never failed to raise England's morale. His figures are proof of his great value to England.

He had an impish sense of humour and his combination of mimicry and clowning endeared him to crowds all over the world – even more so in fact than in his own country. After a long defensive innings he would suddenly decide to reach his hundred with a six. I saw him do it twice in Tests.

He was a sound fielder anywhere with a high accurate return to the wicket. He was a far better leg-spinner than his figures show – he even bowled the flipper – and he was grossly underbowled by a succession of Test captains.

Later as manager and assistant manager of England teams he acted as coach, father confessor and deflater of any awkwardness of temperament. He himself was a sensitive, conscientious and a worrier, and bottled up increasing tensions. He recovered from one heart attack on the field of play in a 6-a-side match at Melbourne. But he died suddenly from another attack whilst assistant manager to Alan Smith on that difficult tour of West Indies in 1981.

The pressure had proved too much for him and England and the world of cricket were robbed of a much loved player, whose loyalty, fighting spirit and dedication had served his country so well.

BATTING

	Innings	Not Out	Highest Score	Runs	Average	Hundreds
Career	831	136	256	31,714	45.63	76
Tests (82)	131	15	256	6,806	58.67	20

1968: Gary Sobers

Barbados, South Australia, Nottinghamshire and West Indies
Born: 28 July 1936. Knighted 1975
Career: 1952/3–74

The greatest all-rounder the world of cricket has ever seen? Impossible to judge, of course, without having seen W G Grace. But surely no one can ever have been better? He qualified as one of the first three batsmen in the world, possibly the best opening bowler with the new ball and had no superior as a leg slip. In addition, of course, he bowled orthodox left arm, or chinaman and googlies. The power of his strokes had to be seen to be believed. He really hammered the ball instead of just stroking it, and there were few better sights than one of his sizzling off-drives through extra cover or his crashing hook to the leg boundary. His movements were those of a giant cat – he slunk over the ground, light of foot, and his eye and body were in perfect co-ordination. He holds the highest Test score of 365 not out and only Gavaskar and Boycott have scored more Test runs. When you ally this to his 235 wickets and 110 catches, can you wonder that he is described by modern followers of cricket as the greatest ever? He himself is modest and charming with a delightful sense of humour. As captain he was shrewd, if sometimes unorthodox in the field, but he always played to win and his declarations, without being give-aways, usually offered the opposition a good chance if they cared to take it. If there is ever a better cricketer than Gary, I hope I shall be alive to see him.

BATTING

	Innings	Not Out	Highest Score	Runs	Average	Hundreds	Catches
Career	609	93	365*	28,315	54.87	86	407
Tests (93)	160	21	365*	8,032	57.78	26	109

BOWLING

	Balls	Runs	Wickets	Average	Best Bowling
Career	–	28,941	1,043	27.74	9 for 49
Tests	21,599	7,999	235	34.03	6 for 73

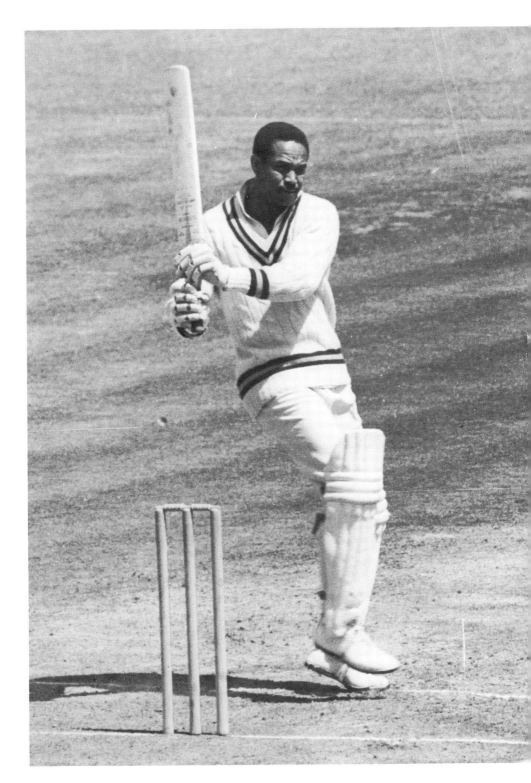

1969: Eddie Barlow

Transvaal, Eastern Province, Western Province, Derbyshire and South Africa.
Born: 12 August 1940
Career: 1959/60–82/3

Although he later wore contact lenses, with his ample figure Eddie had a look of Billy Bunter about him. But there the fun stopped. He was one of the keenest competitors in cricket. He never gave up and always wanted to be in the game, whether opening the batting, snapping up difficult chances at first slip or coming on as first or second change bowler to pick up cheap wickets. As a batsman he was full of guts and unintimidated by the fastest bowlers. In his early days he was apt to slash at the ball outside the off stump and scored quite a few runs over slips' heads. Later he took fewer risks and made more runs. He was especially strong off the back foot and a splendid cutter and hooker. As a fast medium bowler swinging the ball away from the bat, he looked a pushover to spectators. But time and time again he came on in a Test match when his side badly needed a wicket and promptly took 3 wickets in the space of an over or two. He did this three times in Tests in Australia, twice in South Africa, and again in England for the Rest of the World when at Headingley he took 4 wickets in 5 balls, including the hat-trick. A truly remarkable cricketer, who, because of his character played far above his natural potential. He revitalized Derbyshire cricket after taking over their captaincy in 1976.

BATTING

	Innings	Not Out	Highest Score	Runs	Average	Hundreds
Career	493	28	217	18,212	39.16	43
Tests (30)	57	2	201	2,516	45.74	6

BOWLING

	Balls	Runs	Wickets	Average	Best Bowling
Career	–	13,786	571	24.14	7 for 24
Tests	3,021	1,362	40	34.05	5 for 85

1970: Tom Graveney

Gloucestershire, Worcestershire, Queensland and England
Born: 16 June 1927
Career: 1948–71/2

The most graceful of all post-war batsmen, and always a pleasure to watch, even in defence. He played all strokes with elegance, style and perfect timing, and whenever possible off the front foot. He got many of his runs by 'working' the ball on the leg-side. An unmistakable figure as he went out to bat. He had a gliding walk with right shoulder dipped below the level of the left, and his hand tugging at the extra large peak of his cap.

His early Test career was inconsistent and selectors and some captains felt that he had not got the right temperament to 'get stuck in'. He often seemed to give his wicket away when well set. As a result he was not selected as often as he should have been, but made a dramatic return to the Test scene in 1966 at the age of thirty-nine. Strangely he found runs harder to get against Australia than the West Indies, against whom he was a prolific scorer.

He was a useful change bowler with his high leg-breaks and was a good safe catcher and fielder, though not as speedy as some. He once even kept wicket in a Test substituting for an injured Godfrey Evans. It was against South Africa at Old Trafford in 1955, and the first ball he tried to take from Frank Tyson broke his little finger!

He was a Gloucestershire man born and bred and played for them for twelve years, being their captain for the last two. There was then 'a little local difficulty' and he left and went to Worcestershire for another ten years, ending up as *their* captain. Not so many people know that due to an injury to Colin Cowdrey, he also once captained England – at Headingley against Australia in 1968.

A cheerful friendly personality who without ever appearing to be run-hungry has still scored more runs *since the war* than any other batsman, though at the end of 1985 Geoff Boycott was breathing down his neck – just 359 runs behind him!

BATTING

	Innings	Not Out	Highest Score	Runs	Average	Hundreds
Career	1,223	159	258	47,793	44.91	122
Tests (79)	123	13	258	4,882	44.38	11

1971: Barry Richards

Natal, Hampshire, South Australia and South Africa
Born: 21 July 1945
Career: 1964/5–82/3

The most technically perfect of all Test batsmen of recent years. All his strokes on either side of the wicket, off the front or back foot, were right out of any coaching manual. Unlike most modern batsmen he used his feet to all bowlers, and advanced down the pitch in an insolent way to even the fastest of them – just as George Gunn used to do. He seldom waited to play himself in and if the first ball was a half volley he hit it for 4. He tended to become careless, however, after a certain time at the crease and one got the feeling that he got bored unless being fully tested by the highest class bowling. He was ideal for any schoolboy to copy, from his side-on stance at the wicket with his chin tucked into his left shoulder to the way in which he took up and brought down his bat – in a dead straight line. He was a very good catcher near the wicket, could turn an off-break quite viciously off a very short run. Definitely one of the few batsmen whom it was worth travelling half-way across the world to see and would undoubtedly have made many more runs had he had the incentive of playing in Test cricket.

BATTING

	Innings	Not Out	Highest Score	Runs	Average	Hundreds
Career	576	58	356	28,358	54.74	80
Tests (4)	7	0	140	508	72.57	2

1972: Mike Procter

Natal, Western Province, Rhodesia, Gloucestershire and South Africa
Born: 15 September 1946
Career: 1965–83/4

After the retirement of Gary Sobers, there is no doubt in my mind that 'Proccers' took over the title of the best all-rounder in the world. Bowling from a run of inordinate length his fastest ball was faster than anyone else's. He galloped up at a tremendous pace, fair hair bobbing up and down, and delivered the ball with a whirlwind action off the wrong foot. There was none of the classical body swing of a Lindwall or a Trueman. It was primarily an arm action and he could only achieve this great pace because he was so strongly built and so superbly fit. He was an awe-inspiring sight from the pavilion as he ran up. What he must have been like to the batsmen I dread to think! They had long enough to contemplate! Like most really fast bowler he did not do much with the ball. All he basically had to do was to bowl fast and straight, though he did vary his angle of delivery by using the crease, sometimes bowling wide from the return crease or even going round the wicket, from where he even obtained lbw decisions.

Had he not been an all-rounder I think he could have become one of the top five batsmen in the world. With his superb eye and great strength he could devastate any attack and at the same time play copy-book cricket with all the classical strokes. And, a rarity these days, he played *straight*. When he wasn't bowling he 'took it easy' in the slips, where I have seen him pick up some superlative catches with consummate ease.

It all seems unfair, doesn't it, that one man should have had so much. But the good thing about it is that he was also a very nice person. He just happened to love playing cricket, and to be supremely good at it. Lucky Gloucestershire, who became a great team under his captaincy where he showed deep sympathy and understanding. Alas, he was caught up in the Packer affair, which was not only sad but unfair considering that he could not play Test cricket for his country anyhow.

BATTING

	Innings	Not Out	Highest Score	Runs	Average	Hundreds
Career	663	57	254	21,904	36.14	48
Tests (7)	10	1	48	226	25.11	0

116

BOWLING

	Balls	Runs	Wickets	Average	Best Bowling
Career	–	27,249	1,407	19.36	9 for 71
Tests	1,514	616	41	15.02	6 for 73

1973: Colin Cowdrey

Kent and England
Born: 24 December 1932
Career: 1950–76

Has played in more Tests than any other cricketer, making the most runs after Gavaskar, Boycott and Sobers, and taking the most catches after Greg Chappell. Given the initials M.C.C. by his cricket-loving father, he was trained from birth to captain England and did so twenty-seven times. Although heavily built he was a natural ball player, with an exceptional eye and lightness of foot. He started as a leg-break bowler for Tonbridge at Lord's at the age of thirteen but he soon lost the art and became a batsman in the classical mould. He had all the known strokes plus a sort of sweep of his own, which was really a straight drive in reverse down to long leg. A very good player of fast bowling, he always seemed to have plenty of time in which to play the ball – a sure sign of class. Although his figures prove his success, one has the feeling that but for his temperament he *could* have been the greatest batsman of them all. When in the mood he was a class above everyone else, but all too often he appeared an ordinary player. The fault lay in his total disbelief in his own ability. Even after 114 Tests he still experimented with new grips on the bat handle or a new stance at the wicket. Nor was his mood consistent. He could start off brilliantly and then for no reason shut up shop. He made most of his catches at first slip where at his best he could be compared to Hammond or Simpson. As a captain he could be disappointingly defensive. But on tour in the West Indies he created a real team spirit just as he had done in his fifteen years of captaining Kent, whom he led to the County Championship in their centenary year, 1970. The only player to tour Australia six times, being vice-captain on four occasions.

BATTING

	Innings	Not Out	Highest Score	Runs	Average	Hundreds	Catches
Career	1,130	134	307	42,719	42.89	107	638
Tests (114)	188	15	182	7,624	44.06	22	120

1974: Greg Chappell

South Australia, Queensland, Somerset and Australia
Born: 7 August 1948
Career: 1966/7–83/4

The middle of the three Chappell brothers, Ian, Greg and Trevor – grandchildren of Vic Richardson on their mother's side. Greg was one of the top Australian batsmen. I was lucky enough to see his first Test innings of 108 at Perth in the 2nd Test in 1970. With Ian Redpath he rescued Australia, putting on 219 for the 6th wicket. After a slow first 50, Greg scored his last 60 in only 13 overs and his on-driving was some of the best I have ever seen. He appeared then largely a leg-side player, but subsequently he has gained a complete repertoire of strokes all round the wicket, which we saw produced to perfection in his brilliant 131 against England at Lord's in 1972. He was very correct, and an upright commanding player, with the will to win – not at *all* costs maybe – but certainly to the extent of giving no mercy nor quarter to his opponents. In other words, although he loved cricket as a game, he played it hard. In addition, he was a magnificent fielder in any position but especially in the covers or as a close catcher anywhere near the wicket. His medium pace bowling was an added benefit to his side as like d'Oliveira he was a useful wrecker of partnerships. He left his native South Australia to captain Queensland where he was a selector until 1977, and gave a tremendous shot in the arm to cricket in that State. He took over the captaincy of Australia from his brother Ian, and except for a break during the time with Packer, went on to captain them 48 times, a record for his country. He was an astute captain who played the game hard, but in a sporting way – with the exception of course of his infamous instruction to his brother Trevor to bowl an underarm grub to McKechnie when New Zealand needed six to win off the last ball of the 1981 one-day International at Melbourne. It was a decision he has always regretted. He continued to be the master batsman until he retired in 1984, scoring more Test runs than any Australian and getting more catches than any other Test player.

BATTING

	Innings	Not Out	Highest Score	Runs	Average	Hundreds	Catches
Career	542	72	247*	24,535	52.20	74	376
Tests (87)	151	19	247*	7,110	53.86	24	122

BOWLING

	Balls	Runs	Wickets	Average	Best Bowling
Career	–	8,717	291	29.95	7 for 40
Tests	5,227	1,913	47	40.70	5 for 61

1975: Dennis Lillee

Western Australia and Australia
Born: 18 July 1949
Career: 1969/70–83/4

I have seen all the really great fast bowlers since the last war – Lindwall, Miller, McKenzie, Davidson, Adcock, Heine, Hall, Trueman, Statham, Tyson, Holding and Roberts. And quite a few *before* the war too, including Gregory, Larwood, and Farnes. But Dennis Lillee, in my opinion, could match them all for speed, and I'm afraid surpass them all with his language on the field – Freddie Trueman included! It is difficult to judge pace unless one has played against it, but Lillee's fastest ball was certainly as quick as any, with the possible exception of Tyson in Australia in 1954–55. In his run-up, action, change of pace and movement in the air and off the pitch, he was nearer to Lindwall than anyone, and there could be no higher compliment than that! With his long dark hair and Mexican-style moustache he must have been an awesome sight to the batsman. One of his greatest assets in his early days was his willingness to learn and take advice, and he also gained most valuable experience of movement and swing during a season in the Lancashire League with Haslingden. Like all the great fast bowlers, he learnt how to pace himself and not tear away at full speed the whole time. He had wonderful stamina and courage as proved when in 1973 four stress fractures in his back looked like ending his career. But after six weeks in plaster and a long spell of remedial exercises, he returned first as a batsman and then back to his full pace in time to play against Mike Denness's MCC team in 6 Tests and take 25 wickets. With Jeff Thomson as his partner, he proved how helpful it is for fast bowlers to hunt in pairs, and between them they annihilated not only England but the outstanding batting strength of the West Indies in the following year. On the fast bouncy Australian pitches – especially Perth and Sydney – I honestly feel that as a pair they were virtually impossible to master. They both bowled too many unnecessary bouncers, but Lillee was too fine a bowler to need to resort to this. He was a good fielder and became a useful tail-end batsman. He is the greatest wicket-taker in Test cricket, though Ian Botham is breathing down his neck! He showed his greatness as a bowler by the way he adjusted his methods to suit his increasing years. He rationed his really fast ball and altered his run-up to suit the conditions. Some of his histrionics and bad behaviour on the field were inexcusable, especially his swearing at the batsmen he

'hated'. But off the field he was a different person, friendly and likeable.

BOWLING

	Balls	Runs	Wickets	Average	Best Bowling
Career	–	19,317	845	22.86	8 for 29
Tests (70)	18,467	8,493	355	23.92	7 for 83

1976: Alan Knott

Kent and England
Born: 9 April 1946
Career: 1964–85
Known to everyone as 'Knotty'.

They say there are no personalities in the game today. Well, look under the peak of this man's Kent or England cap and you would see a pair of piercing brown eyes behind which lies a real character. Off the field he was quiet of manner and speech but with each remark accompanied by a wicked twinkle from those eyes. He took a long time to prepare himself for the field and was meticulous about the cleanliness and efficiency of his equipment. You would usually see him last out of the dressing-room hurriedly pulling on his gloves. He only drinks an occasional glass of wine, does not smoke, likes to go to bed early, and is a fanatic about physical fitness. Many of you will have seen him exercise behind the stumps as he swayed sideways, swinging his arms, bending his knees, and touching his toes.

He worried about his health and thought he was in danger of stiffening up unless he did those exercises. On the field he exuded energy and dynamism and was just like a 'Jack in the Box' as he crouched behind the stumps ready to 'take off' in any direction to make a miraculous catch or save a certain four byes. In his day he was the greatest wicket-keeper in the world and ranks with the best of all time. He broke Godfrey Evans' record of 219 Test dismissals and later became the first wicket-keeper to take 250 wickets in Test cricket. He was also the only keeper to make two centuries in Tests between England and Australia. Safe, swift, sure, and at the same time, spectacular, it is inevitable that he should be compared with Godfrey Evans.

I have watched them both intently with admiration, disbelief, and I must admit, with envy. I would say that Knott was more consistent than Evans but through lack of opportunity did not prove himself as Evans' equal at standing up to medium-fast bowling. Evans had to deal with the whiplash of Bedser. But standing back to the fast bowlers or up to the spinners there is nothing to choose between them. There can surely never have been anyone better than either of them. Knott, like Evans, was also a greater taker of bad returns and made the poor thrower look good by going to meet the ball on the full pitch. He also had the same energy and good humour as Evans did at the end of a long, hot tiring day. Knott had one peculiarity – he found it easier to take some returns from the field one-handed,

plucking the ball out of the air like a conjurer. He made it look easy but budding wicket-keepers, please don't copy. Knott could do it, but you may not!

His batting improved to such an extent that he came close to being an England batsman without his wicket-keeping. Like Evans he could defend or attack, whichever the situation demanded. At one time he found it difficult to play an innings with a mixture of both – and it had to be one or the other. But later he blossomed out. He always used his feet well but mostly to defend, picking up most of his runs from the cut. But he became the greatest improviser ever seen in Test cricket. His sweeps – often from outside the off stump! His cuts – often off the middle stump! His drives – sometimes hitting sixes over mid-off! Knott and Evans had one other thing in common. They were entertainers who loved their cricket and some-how shared their enthusiasm with the crowd. None of us who saw him will ever forget Evans, and everyone who watched Knott keeping wicket saw a great artist who, I believe, became the undis-puted equal or even master of them all.

After his defection to Packer in 1978 he returned to play six more Tests, four against West Indies in 1980, and two against Australia in 1981. Had he not had an ankle injury he might well have played for England again in 1985. It was the year when he finally retired, but he was keeping wicket as well as ever.

BATTING

	Innings	Not Out	Highest Score	Runs	Average	Hundreds
Career	745	134	156	18,105	29.63	17
Tests (95)	149	15	135	4,389	32.75	5

WICKET-KEEPING

Career	1,344 Dismissals (1,211 caught, 133 stumped)
Tests	269 Dismissals (250 caught, 19 stumped)

1977: Graeme Pollock

Eastern Province and South Africa
Born: 27 February 1944
Career: 1961/2–

One of the most exciting batsmen in the world – a left-hander who has often been compared to Frank Woolley. In fact, whereas Woolley stroked the ball away, Pollock power-drives it or crashes it through the covers. He uses a very heavy bat – 2lb 12oz – and his driving off front or back foot on either side of the wicket is out of this world. He is also a grand cutter and hooker. Early on he appears vulnerable to the ball which leaves him on or just outside his off stump (but what batsman isn't?). Like Hammond he is also said to be weaker off his leg stump. In fact in South Africa the Australians tried to contain him by bowling at his legs to a leg-side field. It certainly stopped his scoring rate but he never looked unhappy. A tall fair-haired giant he has a shambling gait and is basically rather a lazy character. A safe catcher and fielder and also bowls the odd leg-break. A natural at other games, he has had trouble with his right eye, and tried playing in glasses. But now plays as well as ever without them.

BATTING

	Innings	Not Out	Highest Score	Runs	Average	Hundreds
Career	414	51	274	19,813	54.58	60
Tests (23)	41	4	274	2,256	60.97	7

1978: Vivian (Viv) Richards

Leeward Islands, Combined Islands, Somerset and West Indies
Born: 7 March 1952
Career: 1971/2–

By the end of the 1977 season he had undoubtedly taken over as the best batsman in the world, following the slight falling off in Greg Chappell's form, and with Barry Richards missing the incentive of Test cricket. Viv sprang upon the Test world in 1974. He has succeeded against all types of bowlers – the devastating speed men of Australia, the wily spinners of India, and the swing and seam bowlers of England. His appetite for runs matches that of Don Bradman in the 'thirties. A hundred to him is just a stepping stone to bigger things. In the Oval Tests in 1976, only tiredness seemed to prevent him beating Gary Sobers' 365 not out. Amassing big scores is not the only likeness between the two. The manner in which Viv consistently smashes the bad ball to the boundary or places the good one between fielders for ones and twos, enables him to score at just as fast a rate as Bradman ever did. He possesses all the strokes and his execution of them is perfect. His timing of the ball is masterly and, like all the great players, he plays the ball a fraction later than the average batsman. In one way he *does* differ from the Don. He enjoys hitting sixes, whereas the Don believed in keeping the ball on the ground, whenever possible. He is also far more unorthodox than the Don and takes many more risks. He thinks nothing of hooking a short ball outside the off-stump over square leg for six! He is a fine fielder anywhere with a lethal throw and his off-breaks have improved so much that West Indies can afford to play only one genuine spinner. He has taken over the captaincy from Clive Lloyd and it will be interesting to see whether it affects his form. I bet it won't! I am sure that he will continue to be the world's greatest batsman for several years more. With the peak of his cap pointing up to the sky he enjoys his cricket and is friendly and likeable.

BATTING

	Innings	Not Out	Highest Score	Runs	Average	Hundreds
Career	572	38	322	26,841	50.26	86
Tests (77)	116	7	291	5,889	54.02	19

1979: Geoffrey Boycott

Yorkshire, Northern Transvaal and England
Born: 21 October 1940
Career: 1962–

The enigma of post-war cricket. Handicapped by wearing glasses, with little natural talent or athleticism, by self-discipline and dedication, he made himself into a great defensive batsman and a hungry accumulator of runs. By constant hours of practice he gradually learnt every known way of defending his wicket. His defensive technique is faultless. He also added a few comparatively safe scoring strokes. With his enormous appetite for runs, he became the greatest run-getting machine since Don Bradman. But what a contrast! Geoff could never be classed as a great batsman in every sense of the word, because he seldom tries to dictate to the bowler. Only once did I see him really take an attack apart – in the Gillette Final of 1965 when he scored a brilliant 146 against Surrey. As a result he always takes too long to accumulate his runs. The sad fact is that the more runs he makes for Yorkshire, the less likely are they to have the time to win. Both in Test and County cricket while he blocks away for hours, his fellow batsmen have to take risks to try to keep the score moving. He honestly feels that since he is the best batsman in the side, he must stay at the wicket regardless. If quick runs were needed, the others must get them. If there was a danger of a run-out, the other batsman should make the sacrifice. And alas there *were* many run-outs!

All this has not endeared him to his team-mates. In addition he is a natural loner, dedicated to cricket. He keeps himself tremendously fit. He drinks little, likes his sleep, and on tours, instead of lying on the beach on the day off, would get local boys to bowl at him for hours in the net. He just loves to bat, and occupy the crease. His whole playing career has been taken up with rows, disputes, and arguments and he even exiled himself from Test cricket for three years.

He has always been most friendly to me and I have always felt that he hungered, not just for runs, but for friendship. But he was not prepared to make the necessary sacrifices and adjustments which that entails.

Whatever the feelings of his fellow players he can point to an enormous and adoring following from ordinary Yorkshiremen. But perhaps like him, they are too apt to judge their heroes by the runs in the book. Anyway there is no disputing that on figures alone Geoff is

a world beater and that his defensive technique can be copied by every aspiring young cricketer.

BATTING

	Innings	Not Out	Highest Score	Runs	Average	Hundreds
Career	994	161	261*	47,434	56.94	149
Tests (108)	193	23	246*	8,114	47.72	22

1980: Sunil Gavaskar

Bombay, Somerset and India
Born: 10 July 1949
Career: 1966/7–

Has scored more runs (8,654)* and more hundreds (30) in Test cricket than any other player and still with an average of over 50. A mixture of Bradman and Boycott combining the best of both. Smaller than either of them (5'4¾") he has their concentration, consistency and love of accumulating runs. As an opening batsman for most of his career he has had to counter the speed and bounce of the world's fastest bowlers. In spite of his height he has coped with all the problems which that brings to a batsman. He has a perfect defensive technique and is a good runner between the wickets. He uses his feet and is a fine driver of the ball. But unlike many short batsmen does not favour the hook – which eliminates one way of getting out. Add all these skills to his great powers of patience and concentration and his massive number of runs are easily explained.

His captaincy of India does not seem to have affected his batting, though in later years he has tended to bat lower down in the order, leaving some of the initial 'flak' to the younger batsmen. In a cricket crazy country he is a No. 1 Hero, and receives film star treatment and adulation wherever he goes.

BATTING

	Innings	Not Out	Highest Score	Runs	Average	Hundreds
Career	515	57	340	23,539	51.39	74
Tests (106)	185	14	236*	8,654	50.60	30

* Since September 1985 he has increased his total to more than 9,000 runs, including two more centuries.

1981: Ian Botham

Somerset and England
Born: 24 November 1955
Career: 1974–

What can one say about this cricketing Colossus? Certainly the best all rounder since Gary Sobers. Certainly the best hitter of a cricket ball I have ever seen. A magnificent fielder and catcher anywhere, but especially at second slip, standing a yard or more in front of the others. Has been a great out-swing bowler, and sometimes still is. In 1985 was used as a strike opening bowler. As his figures show, no matter what he bowls, or how expensive he is, he has become the second greatest wicket taker in Test cricket – now only twelve wickets behind Dennis Lillee.*

In some ways he is the ideal player for a captain to have on his side. He plays to win, but loses gracefully. He always tries and never gives up. He likes to be in the game the whole time, and never wants to give up bowling. But this can produce problems for a captain. Ian is a very strong personality who is apt to take over a side, both on the field and in the dressing room. This undoubtedly made things difficult for Gower when he first took over the captaincy.

As a batsman he is tremendously strong and uses a very heavy bat. He hits beautifully straight, but can never resist a challenge from a bowler, especially when challenged to hook. If a fielder is placed at deep square-leg, he will try to hit the next short ball over his head. Sometimes of course he fails and holes out. Similarly in his many attempts to drive a bowler straight for six, the occasional ball will go off the edge of the bat and he will be caught at cover. Some people then wring their hands and say 'Fancy playing a shot like that in a Test', (especially when he tries the reverse sweep through the slips!). But that is Botham. More than any other cricketer in the world he can turn a game round in a matter of half an hour or so. As proof of this there is no need to look further than that remarkable 1981 series against Australia.

After 1981 he seemed to lose his bowling action and rhythm due to overweight, and the famous outswinger disappeared. Even so he still wanted to bowl, but often bowled far too short and far too long – Gower in his early days as captain finding it very difficult to prise the ball away from him. But in 1985 after a winter away from cricket he seemed to have recovered his old zest and swing. He was fitter and slimmer and ran up with all the old speed. And a more confident Gower used him in shorter spells as an opening strike bowler.

* After England's 1986 tour of the West Indies Botham is only one wicket behind Lillee.

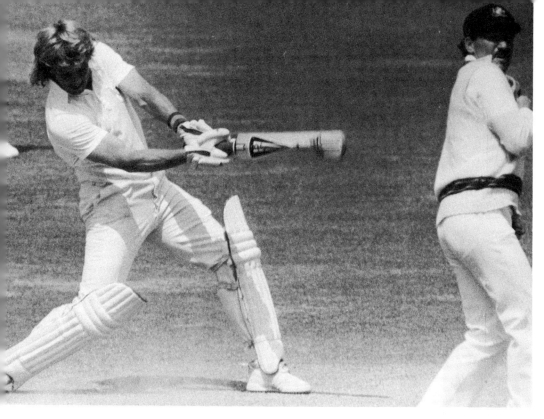

There is no reason why he should not go on to take 400 Test wickets, to hit countless more sixes (he hit a record 80 in 1985) and to play some more of those incredible swashbuckling innings. He is a tremendous crowd puller and has become the biggest earner the game has ever known. Let's hope that he not only continues to make the best of his talent, but also remembers that he is only one in a team of eleven. One final thought. We must pray that his magnificent walk from John O'Groats to Land's End on behalf of the charity Leukaemia Research has not done irreparable harm to his legs – such an essential part of a bowler. But full credit to him for being prepared to take the risk of further weakening his already suspect knees and ankles for such a worthy cause. Countless children will for ever be grateful to him for the thousands of pounds he collected on the way.

BATTING

	Innings	Not Out	Highest Score	Runs	Average	Hundreds	Catches
Career	414	31	228	13,437	35.08	29	246
Tests (79)	125	3	208	4,409	36.13	13	92

BOWLING

	Balls	Runs	Wickets	Average	Best Bowling
Career	–	22,957	896	25.62	8 for 34
Tests	18,391	9,046	343	26.37	8 for 34

1982: Bob Taylor

Derbyshire and England
Born: 17 July 1941
Career: 1960–84

The ideal professional and one of the best wicket-keepers ever to play Test cricket. Due to Alan Knott he had to wait eleven years before he played in his first Test. It was in New Zealand in 1971 and then only because Ray Illingworth asked Knott to stand down so as to give Bob his due reward for his skill and loyalty. During the years that he was understudy to Knott he never complained but just considered himself lucky to be chosen to tour with an England team.

From 1977 when Knott 'defected' to Packer, Bob became England's automatic choice behind the stumps. As a wicket-keeper he had a beautiful pair of hands and was quiet and undemonstrative. Both standing up or standing back he was a perfect model for young wicket-keepers to follow. Throughout his fifty-seven Tests a miss by him made headlines in the sports papers.

With his white sun hat turned up in front only partly covering his grey hair, he showed remarkable agility and caught some brilliant diving catches – tumbling like a parachutist landing. Godfrey Evans was famous for the way he encouraged his team-mates, raising their spirits and morale at the end of a long hot day in the field. Bob, in his own quiet way, did the same. At the end of an over he would often chase after a perspiring fast bowler and pat him on the back. Like Godfrey, he made bad returns to the wicket look good and always applauded a fielder for an accurate throw over the stumps.

Off the field he was the perfect tourer, uncomplaining, cheerful, helpful to the other players and loyal to the manager. He attended every function whether official or unofficial and was given the nick-name 'Chat' because of the way he chatted up his hosts and the other guests. He was such a perfectionist that he gave up his short captaincy of Derbyshire, because he felt it was affecting his wicket-keeping.

His batting was orthodox and useful and he played several defensive roles in Test partnerships. But he was, I think, rightly considered one of the 'tail'. Towards the end of his career he sadly became disillusioned with some of the behaviour and trends of his younger colleagues. His own standards as a keeper and a man remained at the highest peak until he retired in 1984.

BATTING

	Innings	Not Out	Highest Score	Runs	Average	Hundreds
Career	878	167	100	12,040	16.93	1
Tests (57)	83	12	97	1,156	16.28	0

WICKET-KEEPING

Career	1,646 Dismissals	(1,471 caught, 175 stumped)
Tests	174 Dismissals	(167 caught, 7 stumped)

1983: Clive Lloyd

Guyana, Lancashire and West Indies
Born: 31 August 1944
Career: 1963/4–

An unlikely looking athlete with his spectacles, bowed shoulders and shambling gait. In his early days was a superb fielder in the covers, fast and lithe, pouncing on the ball like a cat, and flicking the ball like lightning to the wicket-keeper. Nowadays he is usually found in the slips, where he picks up with nonchalant ease some remarkable catches off his band of fast bowlers.

As a left-handed bat he must rank with the greatest. Tall with a long reach and good eye he bats with a very heavy bat (about 3lb 3oz) which also has a double thick handle. His favourite stroke is the lofted drive which seems to 'sail' out of the grounds so perfect is his timing. But he also deals fiercely with anything short and is a superb hooker. Early in his career the England bowlers thought that he was a sucker for the ball leaving his bat outside the off-stump, early in his innings. But what left-hander has not had that particular difficulty? Like most of the great Test hitters, his defence is rocklike – in spite of so-called groggy knees he has kept his speed and his running between the wickets has brought him many extra runs.

He could be quite a useful medium pace bowler and captained West Indies 74 times. He had a quiet and seemingly casual approach but he brought unity and discipline to his side like his great predecessor Frank Worrell. But underneath it all he was a strong character with high principles and a quiet sense of humour. My only quarrel with him was his tolerance – even if not encouragement – of bouncers and short-pitched bowling. But he clearly thought that the matter was best left in the hands of the umpires. He can anyway point to his remarkable record as captain with 36 victories, 11 of them in succession. Under him too West Indies went 26 Tests without defeat.

BATTING

	Innings	Not Out	Highest Score	Runs	Average	Hundreds
Career	722	95	242*	30,885	49.25	78
Tests (110)	175	14	242*	7,515	46.67	19

1984: Derek Underwood

Kent and England
Born: 8 June 1945
Career: 1963–

One of the greatest left arm bowlers in the history of the game and unique in style. First played for Kent aged 17, and took 101 wickets in both his first two seasons. His pace is near to medium and he cuts rather than spins the ball. The supreme master of length, line and change of pace, he has in the last few years added flight to this formidable armoury which has not only kept class batsmen quiet all over the world, but has earned him 297 Test wickets. On a rain-affected pitch he is practically unplayable, getting the ball to bite and so giving him a nasty lift off the pitch. Surprisingly perhaps, he is not so formidable on a dusty dry pitch, which is cracking up and worn on top. But even when not taking wickets, he can put the brake on even the fastest scoring batsman. He is difficult to 'get at' due to his extra pace, and batsmen find it is difficult to hit him over the top. In addition, the ball which comes in with his arm makes it a big risk to try and cut him. He always likes his first over to be a maiden to give him a superiority complex over the batsmen, and regularly hits the spot with his very first ball. As a batsman he was England's automatic night-watchman for years, possessing a sur-prisingly correct defence technique, plus unlimited guts, which ensures that he gets in line against even the fastest bowlers. But he enjoys a good slog, his favourite stroke being a cow shot over mid-wicket. But more recently he has developed a classic looking off-drive through extra cover, and in 1984 he achieved his life-long ambition of scoring his maiden century – 111 against Sussex at Hastings. Not naturally a quick mover in the field with his rather flat feet, he has become a first-class fielder and safe catcher in the deep with a very good 'arm'. A pleasant cheerful character, and also a great team man who enjoys a fight and never gives up. That made his allegiance to Packer all the more tragic for England and undoubtedly prevented him taking well over 300 Test wickets. He came back to play in twelve more Tests and at the end of the 1985 summer was still wheeling away with his consistent accuracy and occasional devastating spins on a pitch which suits him.

BOWLING

	Balls	Runs	Wickets	Average	Best Bowling
Career	–	47,327	2,368	19.98	9 for 28
Tests	21,862	7,674	297	25.83	8 for 51

1985: Allan Border

New South Wales, Queensland, Gloucestershire and Australia
Born: 27 July 1955
Career: 1976/7–

A small stockily built left-hander who since first appearing for
Australia in 1978 has been their most reliable and consistent middle-
order batsman. Over that time he has gradually developed from a
defensive batsman who punished bad balls into an attacking stroke
player whose aim is first to dominate the bowlers, and then pulverise
them. He reached his peak as captain of Australia in 1985 when he
surprised the cricketing world with his new spirit of attack and
aggression. Especially noticeable was his superb footwork. He had
always been a good cutter and hooker but now he was dancing down
the pitch to drive and not afraid to hit the ball in the air. The result
was a spate of sixes.

The strain of carrying the Australian batting did not seem to
affect his confidence or consistency. He must now rank with all the
top Australian batsmen of the past. He is a good catcher and fielder,
though he did drop an easy catch at mid-wicket during the Headingley Test which would have given Jeff Thomson his 200th Test
wicket. Although not a regular bowler, whenever he put himself on
with his slow left arm spinners he immediately struck a good line
and length and was as economic as any of the other regular bowlers.

As a captain he hardly put a foot wrong and was largely responsible with Gower for the friendly spirit in which the 1985 series was
played. He was a sound tactician and strict disciplinarian on and off
the field. My one complaint against his tactics was the way he placed
five men – occasionally six – on the leg-side to a slow left-armer and
right arm leg-spinner.

BATTING

	Innings	Not Out	Highest Score	Runs	Average	Hundreds
Career	267	41	200	11,821	52.30	33
Tests (72)	127	22	196	5,332	50.78	14

1986: Richard Hadlee

Canterbury, Nottinghamshire, Tasmania and New Zealand
Born: 3 July 1951
Career: 1971/2–

One of five cricketing sons of the old New Zealand captain Wally Hadlee. He was brought up in an atmosphere of cricket, with parental encouragement to play it and enjoy it. He has become the best New Zealand fast bowler ever and with his successful attacking left-handed batting, can also lay claim to be one of their best all-rounders. As a bowler he is not unlike Brian Statham, tall, wiry, longish arms with a whippy and near-perfect sideways action.

He started as a fast bowler with a long run, but due to his playing county cricket for Nottinghamshire he had to learn to conserve his strength and energy. As a result he now bowls off a 12 yard run, and still looks as fast as before – a perfect example of how pointless are the 30 yard run-ups of so many fast bowlers.

He is over six feet tall and his arm comes over high, thus producing bounce and movement off the pitch. With his action, and bowling close to the stumps he has perfected the out-swinger from which he gets many of his wickets. Any aspiring young bowler should copy his methods – good line and length with only the occasional short ball, which often takes the batsman by surprise. In fact on occasions, Richard seems to hypnotise batsmen so that they appear like frightened rabbits caught in a car's headlights.

He's a fine fielder with a good arm, and is a swift mover and safe catcher. Since 1972 he has been indispensable to the New Zealand side and in 1985 against Australia added to his many fine performances with the fourth best-ever analysis for an innings in Test cricket (9 for 37 at Brisbane). By the time this book is out he is sure to have taken over 300 Test wickets and become only the sixth player in Test cricket to do so.* No other New Zealander has taken more than one hundred and sixteen. The figures speak for themselves. What a man to have on your side!

BATTING

	Innings	Not Out	Highest Score	Runs	Average	Hundreds
Career	368	68	210*	8,737	29.12	9
Tests (57)	96	12	103	2,088	24.85	1

BOWLING

	Balls	Runs	Wickets	Average	Best Bowling
Career	–	20,426	1,092	18.70	8 for 41
Tests	14,292	6,341	266	23.83	7 for 23

* He has! (March 1986)

144

1987: David Gower

Leicestershire and England
Born: 1 April 1957
Career: 1975–

The golden boy of English cricket in the late 'seventies and the 'eighties. He slipped through Kent's fingers and was snapped up by the astute Mike Turner of Leicestershire. An intelligent, casual, laid-back character with a nice smile to match his fair good looks and engaging sense of humour. A beautiful mover in the field, very fast with an appearance of gliding over the turf. Especially good in the covers, since becoming captain of England he often fields in the dangerously close silly point position.

As a left-hander he has the ease and grace of Frank Woolley though not his power. But when he is in form his timing is so perfect that he seems to stroke or waft the ball away to the boundary, without any apparent effort. He has had his difficulties and bad patches. At first he was especially vulnerable to the well pitched up ball on his legs, often being caught round the corner at backward square leg. But he overcame that and became the complete batsman. However, when in a bad spell and out of form he has trouble in not moving his feet to the ball on or outside the off-stump. This makes him prone to give catches to the slips. But when in form, with the eye and feet working in perfect co-ordination there is no more graceful, pleasing or entertaining batsman to watch. And added to this he is a good judge of a run, and a fine runner between the wickets.

He was ambitious to become captain of England and to start with he found it a bit difficult. He is basically quiet and unemotional, and obviously found the contrasting aggression and extrovert personality of Botham a bit of a problem. But after the winter tour of India in 1984/85 *without* Botham, he seemed to find new confidence in himself. He operated on the field less and less by committee, restricting his consultations to his trusted lieutenant Mike Gatting.

But early in the 1985 series against Australia one still felt that his batting was suffering because of the extra responsibilities. But then after two tests he magically found his old timing, his feet moved into the right positions, and from then on all was sunshine for England's young blond captain.

BATTING

	Innings	Not Out	Highest Score	Runs	Average	Hundreds
Career	422	38	215	15,590	40.59	34
Tests (76)	129	11	215	5,385	45.63	12

The Main Techniques

THERE ARE many excellent coaching books on cricket mainly written by former Test players. All of them have far better qualifications than myself – a mere commentator – to try to tell young people how to play this wonderful game. But a book like this should have *some* guide on basic techniques. So based on many of the coaching books and on my own experiences of playing cricket I have tried to set out as simply as possible the main essentials which a learner of the game must know. It may even be a help to older players who want to brush up their techniques.

N.B.

1. All the following text and drawings apply to *right*-handed batsmen. The reverse of course applies to left-handers.

2. One essential thing to remember about cricket is that it is a *sideways* game both for batsmen and bowlers. The drawings will illustrate this.

BATTING
The Grip (Figs 1 & 2)
Put the hands close together with the left hand near the top of the handle. The knuckles of the left hand should be facing roughly towards extra-cover, and the V's between the thumb and first fingers on each hand should be in a straight line. The left hand should then rest against the inside of the front pad.

The Stance (Figs 3 & 4)
This must be comfortable, and the stances of the batsmen do therefore vary. But basically the feet should be just apart with the bottom of the bat resting behind the back foot. The two feet should be parallel to the popping crease, the left shoulder pointing down the pitch, with the chin tucked in behind the shoulder. This ensures that both eyes are looking straight down the pitch. The most important thing to remember is to *keep the head still*.

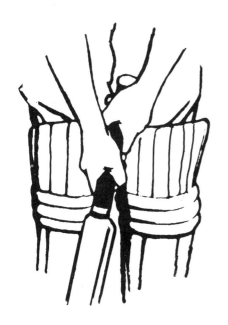

Fig 1

Fig 2

Fig 3

Fig 4

Fig 5

The Back-Lift (Fig 5)
The bat should be taken back as straight as possible⋆ with the leading left arm pushing back over the stumps. The face of the bat should then be facing the offside.

⋆ I say this because many of the great batsmen surprisingly did not take the bat up completely straight. A good example was Don Bradman who took it up towards gully. But he always brought it *down* straight and that is the vital thing that every batsman should do.

Defensive Strokes
The Forward Stroke (Figs 6 & 7)

As for the drives the left foot moves to the pitch of the ball. The batsman's head and eyes are on the line of the ball and with the front knee slightly bent the full face of the bat should make contact with the ball just *in front* of the left foot. The batsman must keep his head down, following the ball right on to the bat. A good defensive batsman is often described as looking as if he's trying to 'smell' the ball.

Fig 6

Fig 7

151

Fig 8

Fig 10

Fig 9

The Back Stroke (Figs 8 & 9)

The right foot should move well back towards the stumps but keep parallel to the popping crease. The bat is taken up as in the back-lift and keeping his head right down the batsman should play the ball virtually sideways on. The top hand should do the work, with the bottom hand only gently gripping the bat. Contact with the ball should be made *in front* of the leading pad.

(*Fig 10*) The back-stroke can be turned into an attacking stroke to a short ball on or outside the off-stump. Instead of cutting, the batsman plays the ball earlier and instead of 'smelling' the ball stands more upright on his toes and follows through after contact. The top hand is still doing most of the work, but the bottom hand will grip the handle tighter and so help give a final push to the stroke.

Attacking Strokes for the Well Pitched-up Ball
The Off-Drive (Figs 11 & 12)

Advance the left foot to the pitch of the ball. The left shoulder should be pointing in the direction in which it is intended to hit the ball, with the left hand controlling this. In advancing towards the pitch of the ball the left foot may leave the ground but the right foot should always remain on the ground. Its rather like a boxer advancing towards his opponent. The head should be kept as still as possible, with both eyes fixed fully on the ball. After hitting the ball the bat should follow through the line of the ball.

Fig 11

Fig 12

Fig 13

Fig 14

The On-Drive (Figs 13 & 14)

More difficult to play than the off-drive as inevitably at one point the batsman has to hit slightly across the line of the ball. But once again the left foot must advance to the pitch of the ball with the left shoulder following. This will mean that the batsman has a more square-on stance and as in the off-drive the head must be kept as still as possible, with the eyes fixed on the ball.

Strokes for the Short-Pitched Ball Outside the Off-stump
The Late Cut (Fig 15)
The back foot must be moved across to the off-stump or outside it with the toe facing in the direction of third man. Both arms are stretched out with the face of the bat pointing to the ground. It is essential to hit the ball *down*, coming down on the ball at about the level of the stumps, with the batsman's weight on the back foot. At the finish of the stroke the batsman's back will have turned and be facing in the direction of the mid-on.

The Square Cut (Fig 16)
This is played earlier than the late cut. This means that the ball will be sent squarer in the direction of cover or backward point. Once again the bat must come *down* on the ball.

An extra ingredient to both these strokes is the roll of the wrists just before contact. This gives genuine cut on the ball and despatches it quicker than when just hitting it down into the ground.

Fig 15

Fig 16

Fig 17

Fig 18

Strokes for the Short-Pitched Ball on the Stumps or Outside Leg stump
The Hook (Figs 17 & 18)
The first move is for the right foot to go right back on the stumps with the toe facing roughly towards mid-off. The batsman will be facing the bowler square on with the bat taken up towards gully. The head must be kept as steady as possible with the eyes never leaving the ball. On contact with the ball the batsman's body pivots round towards the leg side so that he is then facing square leg. On contact the wrists should be rolled over to make sure that the ball is kept down. Too many batsmen – even in Tests – neglect to do this and so hit the ball in the air and get caught. It is undoubtedly a risky stroke to play, but also brings many runs. An important point to remember is to get in position over to the offside outside of the line of the ball as early as possible.

156

Fig 19

Fig 20

The Pull (Figs 19 & 20)
A variation of the hook can be played to a short ball outside the off-stump. This is the pull and aims to hit the ball in the direction between mid-wicket and the stumps at the bowler's end. The batsman's back foot has to move further back across the stumps than in the hook and the batsman will be squarer on to the bowler with the toe of his back foot pointing down the wicket. Once again the wrists must be rolled over to ensure keeping the ball down.

The Leg Glance (Figs 21 & 22)

There is one more basic scoring stroke which can be played to balls on or just outside the leg stump. The ball can be well pitched up or short of a length. This stroke is called the leg glance, and is based on the forward and back strokes in defence. The idea is to deflect the ball down to fine or long leg. Contact with the ball should be made with the bat in front of the front pad and at the moment of impact the wrists turn the bat round, steering the ball down to long leg.

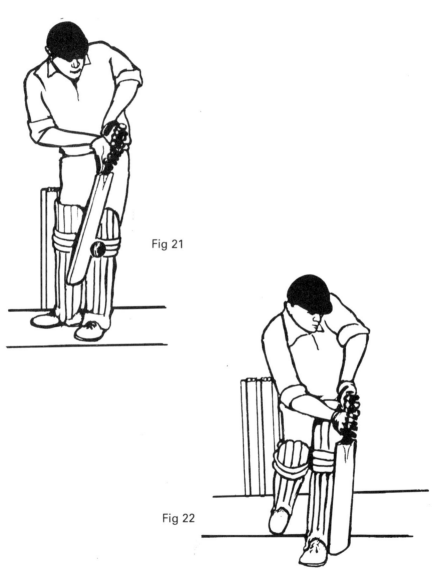

Fig 21

Fig 22

BOWLING

Repeat once again to yourself that cricket is a sideways game. It is the basis of the perfect bowling action.

Figs 23 to 27 give the correct positions from the moment of arrival at the bowling crease until the actual delivery of the ball. Before arriving at the crease a correct run-up is the first thing to get right. It should be a comfortable well-balanced run, starting slowly with a few walking steps and then gradually accelerating as the bowler approaches the stumps. It should be as short as possible. Each bowler must decide on what length suits him depending on his physique, length of stride, etc. Bowlers in first-class cricket tend to take far too long run-ups. But fast bowlers like Michael Holding and Richard Hadlee, both of whom used to take runs of about 30 yards, have proved that they can be even more effective from about 12 yards. Not *quite* so fast perhaps but just as sharp and far more accurate.

The thing to remember is that full momentum should be reached in the last few strides. Then (Fig 23) the bowler jumps in the air off the front foot: the weight is then brought down on the back foot (Fig 24) and the body is poised to touch down on to the front foot for the final delivery stride (Fig 25). The length of the stride will vary depending on the height of the bowler and whether he is bowling fast or slow. A fast bowler running up at speed will inevitably take a longer stride than a slow bowler. Note that the left arm is pointing at the stumps with the bowler's eyes looking along the *outside* of the arm.

Fig 23

159

Fig 24

Fig 25

Fig 26

Fig 27

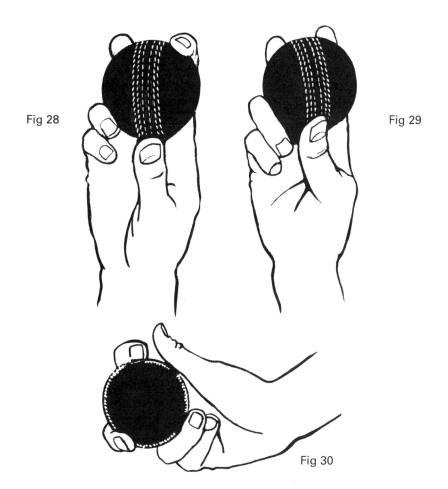

Fig 28

Fig 29

Fig 30

The body is then ready to pivot (see Figs 26 & 27) with the weight transferred fully to the front leg. As the bowler delivers the ball his right arm will come right across his body, and he will complete the pivot with his right leg in the air and his body facing the off side.

So much for the basic bowling action. Now come the various grips necessary for the different types of bowlers.

The Grips
Fig 28 In-swing
The seam is angled in the direction of fine-leg.

Fig 29 Out-swing
The seam is angled in the direction of the slips.

Fig 30 Off-break
The ball is spun clockwise – i.e. the wrist turns from the left to the right. It's just like turning the handle on a door when opening it.

Fig 31 Leg-Spin
The wrist rotates anti-clockwise i.e. from right to left.

Fig 32 Leg-Cutter
A variation of the leg-break used by a medium to fast bowler who is normally an in-swinger. Note that the seam is angled in the direction of the stumps, whereas for the leg-break the seam faces the off and on-side. With the leg-cutter the second finger does the work, *pulling* the ball down from right to left as the wrist rotates. With the leg break the longer middle finger performs this task by *pushing* the ball down.

In the same way there is an off-cutter which is really an off-break with the seam angled in the direction of the stumps and the 1st and 2nd fingers pulling across the seam from left to right.

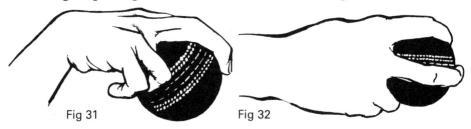

Fig 31   Fig 32

Final words of advice for someone learning to bowl
1. It is hard work, especially for the faster bowlers. It is therefore important to build up stamina. Start with long walks and running finally concentrating on sprinting so as to gain speed for the run-up. But once fit there is no better exercise for a bowler than just bowling, bowling, bowling. It builds up the right muscles, something which P.T. seems to fail to do for a bowler – especially his vital back muscles.

2. To start with, learn to bowl *straight* and to keep a good length. 'A good length' is that no man's land between a short ball and one well pitched up. In other words the batsman must be uncertain whether to play back or to play forward.

3. Once a bowler has achieved accuracy he can experiment with swing or spin, though it is fair to point out that there is a school of thought which thinks a would-be leg spinner should *first* learn to spin the ball, and then go on to perfecting direction and length.

4. Learn to accept the fact that fielders will drop catches off your bowling. They don't do it on purpose, so spare them the dirty look.

5. Whilst on the field of play the batsman is your enemy. Try to find out his weaknesses and exploit them. Above all try to dominate him.

FIELDING

The side which holds all its catches wins most of its matches. A slight exaggeration no doubt, but there is no doubt that a good fielding side can overcome deficiencies in batting and bowling. Good fielding is also something which the less gifted or skilled cricketer can achieve by hard practice and determination. There are again certain basic rules of a fielder. Keep physically fit and try to improve your speed in the field by regular sprinting practice. Concentrate the whole time and never take your eye off the ball, even when running in fast to pick it up. In between deliveries keep your eye on your captain in case he wants to change your position.

Fig 33 Shows the correct stationary position when stopping the ball, with the left knee touching the right ankle as a second line of defence. Note the head still down, with eyes on the ball.

Fig 34 The running approach to the ball, sideways on, with eye on the ball and *both* hands pointing down. When running in fast it is only possible to get the right foot behind the hands as the second line of defence.

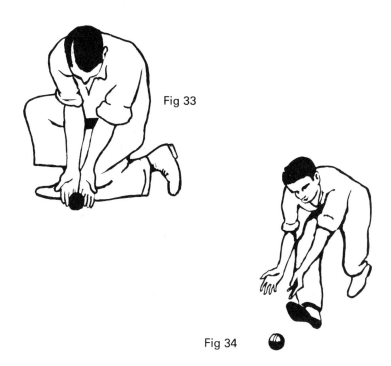

Fig 33

Fig 34

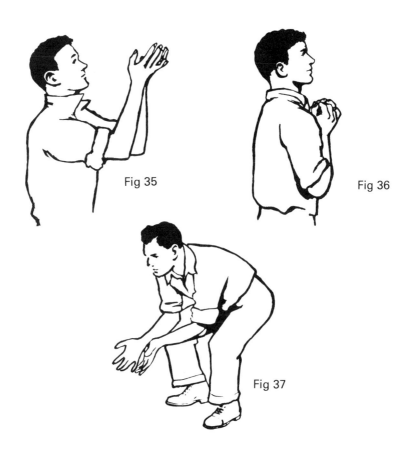

Fig 35

Fig 36

Fig 37

Fig 35 The position for taking a high catch. Eyes as always on the flight of the ball as it comes down. Hands in front of the face with the hands forming a cup. The ball should be caught at about eye level with the hands 'giving' on the point of impact.

Fig 36 Shows how to deal with a ball coming straight at you at a level trajectory. The palms face outwards with fingers pointing upwards.

Fig 37 The correct position for a close fielder, body bending down, hands pointing down. The hands although forming a cup don't quite touch, in case it's necessary to make a one handed catch to a ball passing wide on one side or the other.

Don't rest the elbows on the knees, nor stand with your hands palms downwards on the knees.

There can be no general rule but whenever possible it is always best to try to make a catch with *both* hands.

Fig 38

Fig 39

Figs 38 & 39 Throwing is something which can be achieved by anyone with practice, and it is interesting that the general standard of throwing in first-class cricket is now very high, in contrast with twenty years or so ago. Then only a few members of a side usually had a 'good arm'. Nowadays, everyone seems to be able to throw fast and accurately at the stumps from the usual boundary length of about 75 yards.

The eyes of the thrower should look along the left arm which should be pointed at the stumps. The right arm is drawn well back and as it comes forward the weight of the fielder's body is transferred to the left foot. The throw should have as flat a trajectory as possible. A high throw, however accurate, takes much longer to reach the target.

After releasing the ball the fielder should follow through by pivoting round on his left foot, with the right in the air.

A final warning to young cricketers
Many of you either listen to cricket on the radio or watch it on television. But please be careful not to try to copy everything you see even from the greatest players. There are exceptions to every rule

and some of the top Test players do stray from the orthodox techniques. For example:

1. Viv Richards hits balls from outside the off-stump over square leg for six.

2. Ian Botham may hit a ball on or outside off-stump through the slips with a reverse leg hit – i.e. he turns round quickly and plays it as a left hander.

3. Bob Willis – taker of 325 Test wickets broke all the rules for a fast bowler. He was completely square on when delivering the ball, instead of sideways on.

4. Ian Botham, one of the greatest slip catchers I have ever seen stands with his hands on his knees, instead of cupped as shown in Fig 37.

5. Both Alan Knott and Bob Taylor used deliberately to take returns to the stumps with one hand. Always try to use both.

6. David Gower stands only a yard or so in front of the batsman at silly point. If most people did this they would soon be badly injured.

These are just a few examples of how the great players break the rules. But remember that before they became great they had to learn – and use the basic techniques. Only then could they experiment and extemporise. So continue to enjoy watching them but don't copy *everything* they do.

WICKET-KEEPING

In my opinion the wicker-keeper is the most important man on the field. Wicket-keeping is a difficult art but a most rewarding one. The wicket-keeper is always in the game. More than anyone else he can see exactly what the ball is doing, whether it is turning, swinging or keeping low. He can therefore be of tremendous help to his captain. He can also lift the morale of the fielders by making their returns to the stumps look better than they are. He does this by not standing still behind the stumps and cursing the fielders when their return is out of his reach, either too wide or too short. He will go to meet the ball whenever it is obvious that he will not be able to take it by standing still behind the stumps.

He is also in an excellent position to advise the bowlers of a batsman's weakness, and recommend the type of ball most likely to defeat him. It is obvious that the wicket-keeper must have unflagging concentration right through the day and can never afford to

Fig 40   Fig 41

relax for even one ball. This can be both mentally and physically tiring so that he must always be at the peak of fitness.

It is obviously more difficult to stand up close to the stumps, instead of standing fifteen yards or so back. Fig 40 shows the correct position. In order to get a sight of the ball the right foot should be placed outside the line of the off-stump with the wicket-keeper's head just over or just outside the line of the off-stump. (This will depend on the stance of the batsman). The hands should be pointing *down* with the finger tips just touching the ground, and the gloves cupped so that the little fingers of each hand touch. As for batting, the head should be kept absolutely still with the eyes on the ball from the moment it leaves the bowler's hand.

Fig 41 When taking the ball it is most important to remember *not* to snatch, and to keep the fingers pointing downwards. The keeper should allow the ball to 'enter' his gloves, and to 'give' slightly on the point of impact. This helps prevent bruising. He should remain down as long as possible until he has finally decided on the line the ball will take, and the amount of its bounce. This is easier said than done, especially when the ball is turning or swinging or when the bowler is erratic in his direction. The keeper then has to be prepared to move quickly sideways either to the off or to the leg. But he must never move *backwards*.

This standing up to the stumps is the real wicket-keeper's art, and requires great skill. Standing back is more like goal-keeping and is

167

not half as much fun. But all the basic techniques are still required. Hands pointing down when taking the ball, head still for as long as possible, eyes never leaving the ball. For fast bowlers great agility and anticipation is necessary.

It is often said that wicket keepers are born and not made. It certainly requires instinct to take balls outside the leg stump when standing up to the wicket, since the wicket-keeper's sight of the ball is blocked by the batsman's body. There is no way that he can tell for certain how much the ball will have swung or turned or to judge its bounce. Constant practice is needed to perfect this leg-side taking but the reward of a leg-side catch or stumping is worth all the long hours of hard work.

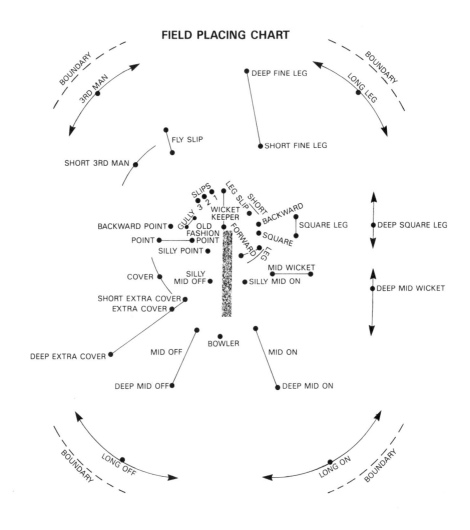

FIELD PLACING CHART

Ten Ways of Getting Out

IN ANY GAME it is important to know and play to the exact laws, and so far as cricket is concerned it is especially important for every player to know when a batsman is 'Out'. The information below, and particularly the diagrams relating to the lbw law should help to clear up any misunderstandings for players, umpires, scorers, and spectators.

1. **BOWLED** (Law 30)
A batsman is out bowled if:
a) His wicket is bowled down even if the ball first touches his bat or his person.
b) He breaks his wicket by hitting or kicking the ball on to it before completing a stroke, or as a result of trying to guard his wicket.
N.B. A batsman is out bowled if the ball is deflected on to his wicket off his person, even though a decision against him for lbw would be justified.

2. **TIMED OUT** (Law 31)
An incoming batsman will be timed out if he *wilfully* takes more than two minutes to come in – the two minutes being timed from the moment a wicket falls until the new batsman steps on to the field of play. On appeal, the umpire at the bowler's end, will give him out if he is satisfied that the delay was wilful.

3. **CAUGHT** (Law 32)
The batsman is out caught if the ball touches his bat or if it touches below the wrist, the hand, or glove, holding the bat, and is then held by a fielder *before* it touches the ground.
N.B. – The fielder must be within the field of play *throughout the act of making the catch*. This starts from the moment the fielder first handles the ball and ends when he has retained full control of the ball – remaining *within the field of play the whole time*.
It is a Fair Catch:
a) If the ball is hugged to the body of the catcher or accidentally

169

lodges in his dress as in the pads of the wicket-keeper. But it is NOT a catch if the ball lodges in a helmet worn by a fielder. In this case the umpire must call 'Dead Ball'.

b) Even if the hand of the catcher touches the ground, provided that the ball does not do so.

c) If the ball is caught after it has been lawfully played a second time by the batsman, so long, of course, that it has not touched the ground before being caught.

d) If the ball touches an umpire, another fielder, or the other batsman, but *not* if the ball has touched a helmet worn by a fielder.

e) If the ball hits an obstruction *within* the boundary full pitch it can be caught as it rebounds, but *not* if the obstruction had previously been agreed as a boundary.

N.B.

a) If a batsman is caught, *no* runs are scored, no matter how many times the batsmen had crossed before the catch was made.

b) When a fielder carrying the ball touches or grounds any part of his person on or over the boundary marked by a line or rope, 6 runs are scored.

c) If a fielder releases the ball *before* he crosses the boundary it may be caught by another fielder. But if the original fielder returns to the field of play and re-catches the ball it is *not* out.

4. HANDLED THE BALL (Law 33)
Either batsman is out if he wilfully touches the ball while in play with the hand not holding the bat, unless he does so with the consent of the opposite side.

N.B. The bowler does not get credit for the wicket.

5. HIT THE BALL TWICE (Law 34)
The batsman is out if after the ball is struck or is stopped by any part of his person, he wilfully strikes it again with his bat or person, except for the sole purpose of guarding his wicket. This he may do with his bat or any part of his person other than his hands.

N.B.

a) The bowler does *not* get credited with the wicket.

b) No runs can be scored from a ball lawfully struck twice except from an overthrow. However, if the fielder has stopped the ball with anything other than his person (i.e. a cap or helmet) then a penalty of 5 runs goes to the batting side.

6. HIT WICKET (Law 35)
The batsman is out, if while the ball is in play:

a) His wicket is broken with any part of his person, dress or equipment as a result of any action taken by him in preparing to receive or in receiving a delivery, or in setting off for his first run, immediately after playing or playing at, the ball.

b) He hits down his wicket whilst lawfully making a second stroke for the purpose of guarding his wicket.

7. LEG BEFORE WICKET (Law 36)

The batsman is out:

a) *Attempting to play the ball*

If he first intercepts with any part of his person, dress or equipment a ball which would have hit the wicket and which has not previously touched his bat or a hand holding the bat, provided that:

(i) The ball pitched in a straight line between wicket and wicket or on the offside of the batsman's wicket or in the case of a ball intercepted full pitch would have pitched in a straight line between wicket and wicket, even if above the level of the bails.

b) *Making no attempt to play the ball*

The batsman is out lbw even if the ball is intercepted *outside* the line of the off-stump if, in the opinion of the umpire, he has made *no* genuine attempt to play the ball with his bat. But if he has tried to make a stroke he is *not out*.

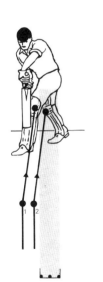  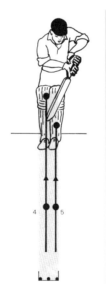 

Ball 1
Not out as batsman made a genuine attempt to play the ball with his bat
Ball 2 – Out

Ball 3
Out as batsman made no genuine attempt to play the ball with his bat

Balls 4 and 5
Out as ball pitched in a straight line between wicket and wicket

Ball 6
Not out as ball pitched outside batsman's leg stump

8. **OBSTRUCTING THE FIELD** (Law 37)

Either batsman is out on appeal if he wilfully obstructs the opposite side by word or action. But if either batsman tries to prevent a catch being made it is the striker who is out. This applies even if the batsman is lawfully trying to guard his wicket.

N.B. The bowler is *not* credited with the wicket.

9. **RUN OUT**

Either batsman is out if in running or at any time while the ball is in play, he is out of his ground, and his wicket is put down. Once a batsman makes his ground he cannot be run out if he then leaves his ground to avoid injury.

N.B.

a) When a no ball has been called the batsman can only be run out if attempting a run.

b) If the batsmen have crossed then the one who runs for the wicket which is put down is out. If they have *not* crossed, then the batsman who has left the wicket which has been put down is the one who is out.

c) If the ball breaks the wicket at the bowler's end neither batsman is run out *unless* the ball has been touched by a fielder *before* the wicket is broken.

d) If a batsman is run out *all* runs run *before* the run which was being attempted, are added to the score.

N.B. The bowler is *not* credited with the wicket.

10. **STUMPED** (Law 39)

The batsman is out if in receiving a ball – not being a no ball – he is out of his ground and the wicket is put down by the wicket-keeper. The wicket-keeper can *not* take the ball in front of the wicket unless it has touched the batsman's person or bat. The wicket-keeper can then stump the batsman from *in front* of the wicket. The batsman can be stumped by the ball rebounding off the wicket-keeper's pads or person or if it is kicked or thrown at the wicket by the wicket-keeper.

A short Quiz

HERE IS A short quiz on the Laws of cricket and Regulations for Test and other first-class cricket. By reading the Ten Ways of Getting Out, The Main Competitions and The Glossary of Terms (see Appendix 1) you should have the necessary information to enable you to answer all the questions. Giving yourself a mark for each correct answer, 35–40 would be very good, 30–34 good, 20–29 average. If you score anything below 20, I suggest you re-read the necessary chapters! You will find the answers in Appendix 5.

1. How many points are awarded for a win in the Britannic Assurance County Championship?

2. May the batsman appeal against the light?

3. What happens when there is one hour left for play on the last day of a Test or other first-class match?

4. A batsman hits the ball in the air over the bowler's head. The ball hits the sight-screen full pitch. The sight-screen is *on* the boundary line. How many runs does the umpire signal?

5. If two or more teams are level at the top of the County Championship at the end of the season, how is the winner decided?

6. When does the ball cease to be dead?

7. How many ways can you be out off a no-ball? Name them.

8. If, while playing the ball, a batsman's cap or helmet falls on to the wicket and knocks off the bails, what decision does the umpire give on appeal?

9. What is the maximum length and width of a cricket bat?

10. How can a batsman be out off a wide?

11. A batsman retires hurt. When may he resume his innings?

12. What are the regulations for the follow-on?

13. What is a King Pair?

14. After how many overs may the new ball be taken in a Test Match?

15. How soon before the start of play must the toss take place?

16. How wide should a cricket pitch be?

17. Can the captain of the opposing side object to the position in which a substitute can field?

18. Can a wicket-keeper stump a batsman if he takes the ball *in front* of the wicket?

19. Is it a no-ball if the bowler's *back* foot just touches the return crease, but does not go over it?

20. Name the circumstances under which a batsman can hit the ball twice *without being out.*

21. Following on the previous question, is there any way a batsman can score runs after legitimately hitting the ball twice?

22. As a bowler runs up to bowl the first ball of his over he pulls a muscle and has to be carried off without having bowled a ball. What action should the umpire take?

23. When does the bowling of short-pitched balls become unfair?

24. Is the batsman out if the ball – without touching the ground – lodges in part of the batsman's or umpire's clothing?

25. A batsman hits the ball which strikes short-leg full pitch on his helmet. From there it rebounds to the wicket-keeper, who catches it. Is the batsman out?

26. Who may polish the ball?

27. Can a captain declare his innings at any time?

28. A batsman hits the ball, and after completing the stroke, sets off on a run. His back foot slips and knocks down the wicket. Is he out?

29. A bowler bowls a bumper and the batsman trying to protect himself flings his bat away. The ball then hits him on his left-hand glove, and is caught by short-leg who claims a catch. Is the batsman out?

30. The batsmen have run two runs. On going for a third, one of them is run out. How many runs are scored?

31. What is a chinaman?

32. What is the height of the stumps?

33. If a fielder on the boundary catches the ball with both hands with both his feet grounded *inside* the boundary and then overbalances and falls over the boundary still with the ball in his hands, is it a catch?

34. The ball has been hit into the outfield and the two batsmen have just completed one run when a dog runs on to the field, picks up the ball, and runs away with it over the boundary. What would you do if you were the umpire?

35. A batsman plays the ball a few feet in front of him. He then stoops, picks up the ball and throws it back to the bowler. Is he out?

36. How can a batsman be 'Timed Out'?

37. An off-break pitches *outside* the line of the off-stump, and hits the batsman's front leg which is also *outside* the line of the off-stump. Provided the ball would have hit the stumps, is the batsman out?

38. When does an umpire signal leg-bye?

39. A ball is signalled a wide by the umpire; the batsman cannot reach it, nor can the wicket-keeper, and the ball goes to the boundary. What is entered in the score-book?

40. A batsman hits the ball back to the bowler in the air. It goes off the bowler's hand on to the wicket at the bowler's end, and breaks it. The non-striker is out of his crease. But the ball still not touching the ground ricochets off the stumps into the hands of mid-on. Is the non-striker run out?

The Tale End

CRICKET IS FUN, not only to play but also to read or talk about. More books on cricket have been written than on any other game. More stories are told about it – many of them true – of events both on and off the field. And behind all these stories laughter is never far away. Few of them are new, but the old ones get reburnished as they are handed down from generation to generation, with the characters sometimes changing. As laughter is such a part of cricket, I thought we should end this part of the book with a few samples of cricket humour. If, when you finally put down the book, you have a smile on your face or laughter in your heart, then you will have caught or recaptured some of the true spirit of cricket.

Harold Larwood, the famous Nottinghamshire and England fast bowler of the 'twenties and 'thirties, was once staying with a friend in the west country and went to watch a village cricket match on the Saturday afternoon. The visiting side were one short and Larwood was pressed to play without anyone knowing who he was. As both umpires came from the home side, who were batting, it was proving somewhat difficult to get them out. In desperation, the captain asked Larwood if he could bowl. He said that he would have a try and, taking a short run, sent down an off-spinner, which the batsman missed and which hit him in the middle of both legs right in front of the wicket. 'Not out', was the reply to the appeal. The next ball, a leg-break, was snicked into the wicket-keeper's hands. Again, 'Not out' was the umpire's decision. Larwood then took his usual run of over twenty yards and send down a thunderbolt which knocked all three stumps out of the ground. Turning to the umpire he said, 'We very nearly had him that time, didn't we?'

While in Australia with the 1962/63 MCC team the Rev. David Sheppard came in for more than his fair share of dropped catches. The story was going around that a young English couple who had settled in Australia were due to have their first-born christened. The husband suggested that it would be nice if they got David Sheppard to do it for them. 'Oh no,' said the horrified wife, 'not likely, he would only drop it!'

He was a very slow bowler and had been hit more or less out of sight when at last the batsman missed a ball which pitched straight – like the others it was devoid of spin – and struck him on the pad. The bowler turned round with a howl of triumph to the umpire and cried, 'How's that?'

'Not out,' said the umpire. The bowler was a very well-bred cricketer and it was not until the end of the over, when he had been hit for three more sixes, that he said to the umpire:

'That one pitched straight, didn't it?'

'Yes.'

'It didn't turn did it?'

'No.'

'He didn't touch it, did he?'

'No.'

'Then why wasn't he out?'

'It wasn't going fast enough to dislodge the bails!'

Bill Reeves, the famous umpire, was seldom at a loss for a reply, but he was struck dumb on one occasion as follows: Surrey were playing Gloucester at Cheltenham, and Alf Gover, Surrey's traditional number eleven, strode to the crease. He took up his stance ready to withstand the onslaught, scorning to take guard. Bill Reeves was never surprised at anything, but noting this somewhat irregular behaviour on Gover's part said, 'Hey, Alf, don't you want your guard?'

'No thanks,' said Alf, 'I've played here before.'

In a village match a visiting batsman was hit high on the chest by the local fast bowler – the village blacksmith. To his surprise the bowler appealed for lbw and to his even greater surprise the umpire gave him out. As he passed the umpire on his way back to the pavilion, the batsman said, 'I couldn't possibly have been out, it hit me in the chest.' 'Well,' said the umpire, 'you look in the local Gazette next Thursday and you'll see you were out right enough.' '*You* look,' snorted the batsman. 'I am the Editor!

W G Grace was batting on a very windy day, and a fast bowler succeeded in getting one past him which just flicked the bails off. The doctor stood his ground and said to the umpire, 'Windy day today, umpire'. Whereupon the umpire replied, 'Very windy indeed, doctor – mind it doesn't blow your cap off on the way back to the pavilion!'

In a village cricket match a very fat batsman came in to bat, and as he was taking up his stance at the wicket the local umpire confided to the visiting bowler: 'We have a special rule for him. If you hit him in front it's lbw. If you hit him behind it's a wide!'

On the day Fred Price made his record of seven catches for Middlesex in a County Championship innings, he was having a drink in the Tavern after the game, when a lady came up to him and said, 'Oh, Mr Price, I did admire your wicket-keeping today, I was so excited, I nearly fell off the balcony.' 'If you had done so, madam,' he replied, 'on today's form I would have caught you too!'

A fast bowler was bowling on a bad wicket, and the opening batsman – who shall be nameless – had to face a number of terrifying deliveries. The first whizzed past his left ear, the second nearly knocked his cap off, and the third struck him an awful blow over the heart. He collapsed and lay on the ground – then after a minute or two got up and prepared to take strike again. The umpire asked him if he was ready – he replied, 'Yes, but I would like the sight-screen moved.'
'Certainly,' said the umpire. 'Where would you like it?' The batsman replied, 'About half-way down the wicket between me and the bowler!'

In a village match a batsman came in wearing only one pad. When this was pointed out to him, the batsman replied, 'Yes, I know, but we only have five pads between us,'
'But,' he was told, 'you've got it on the wrong leg.'
'Oh no,' said the batsman, 'I thought I would be batting at the other end!'

When Frank Tyson was a young man he once went in to bat against a team of first-class cricketers. His form was not very good. He missed the first ball, the next hit him on the pad, he snicked the third, and was clean-bowled by the fourth. As he passed him the umpire said to him, 'Aye, lad, tha was lucky to make nought!'

There is a story about Jack Newman, playing for Hampshire, when he came out to join Lord Tennyson at the wicket in very bad light, and his Lordship called down the wicket to Newman, 'Why don't you appeal against the light, Jack? They won't listen to me.'

To which Newman replied, 'I can hear you, my Lord, but I can't see you . . . where are you?'

The Church of England received a challenge to a cricket match at Lord's from the Roman Catholic Church. The Archbishop of Canterbury was naturally keen to know what sort of chance his side would have before he took up the challenge, so he conferred with the Rev. David Sheppard, who only recommended acceptance if the C. of E. could obtain the services of Ken Barrington. The Archbishop sent for Barrington, specially ordained him, and immediately accepted the challenge.

At half past one on the day of the match he rang up Lord's to ask David Sheppard the score.

'What's our score?'

'I'm sorry, your Grace, but we are forty-four for nine.'

'How dreadful! What happened to the Rev. Kenneth Barrington?'

'Out first ball, I'm afraid.'

'Who is doing the damage, then?'

'A fellow they've got called Father Trueman!!'

At a Yorkshire *v.* Lancashire Roses' match at Sheffield, father arrived early and kept a spare seat for his son, who arrived half an hour after the start of play, breathless and pale with excitement.

'Dad,' he said, 'I've got some terrible news for thee – house is on fire.'

'Aye – '

'Mother's been taken to hospital with bad burns – '

'Aye – '

'And she says she forgot to send insurance money – '

'Aye and I've bad news for thee too – 'Utton's out!'

This is a story about the customary annual match between Durban and Pietermaritzburg. The Mayor and skipper of Durban had represented his side for fifteen years and, during that period, had only captured 2 wickets and made 17 runs, and had never held a catch. The game was duly played in Durban and after a few wickets had fallen, in strode the Mayor of Pietermaritzburg to take strike. All of a sudden he took an almighty swing and the ball went soaring into the heavens straight to the Durban skipper. His apprehension was terrific and in the dying moments he closed his eyes and the ball landed safely in his left hand. His jubilation was fantastic – tossing the ball in the air and then lying down and rolling the ball on his forehead – his first catch ever in such class cricket. He then held the ball aloft to receive the congratulations of his team-mates, but was confronted by a rather irate mid-on who said, 'For God's sake throw the ball back – it was a "No-ball" and the batsmen have run seven already!'

John Snagge, famous BBC broadcaster was once reading the county cricket scores in the news. 'Yorkshire 232 all out. Hutton ill – no I'm sorry – Hutton 111.

In a Middlesex match at Lord's Walter Robins had just completed a very expensive over. He decided it was high time to make a change. He called out to a Middlesex fast bowler. 'Take the next over at this end, Jim.' Umpire Bill Reeves walked up to Robins, who was obviously very annoyed with himself. 'Do you want your sweater sir?' asked Reeves. It was a hot day and the perspiring Robins grumpily replied: 'Keep the bloody thing. And you know what you can do with it.' 'What sir?' said Reeves, examining the Middlesex sweater. 'Swords and all?!'

There was an unorthodox batsman, who could play equally well either right or left-handed. His opponents never knew which it would be until he took up his stance at the wicket. One of them asked him how he decided which way he would play, 'Oh,' he said. 'When I wake up in the morning if my wife is lying on her right side I bat right-handed, if she's on her left side, then I bat left-handed.' 'But what happens if she is lying on her back?' his opponent asked. 'Oh,' he replied, 'in that case I ring up the club to say that I will be an hour late.'

Dr W G Grace had just packed his bag one morning and was ready to go off to play for Gloucestershire, when a lady rushed up to his door and said: 'Can you come quickly, Doctor. I think my twins have got the measles.' 'I'm sorry, ma'am, but I'm already late for my match for Gloucestershire. I'm afraid I cannot come. But contact me at the ground if their temperatures reach 210 for two.'

In a match against Gloucestershire, Brian Close was fielding at forward short leg with Freddie Trueman bowling. Martin Young received a short ball which he hit right in the 'meat' of the bat. It hit Close on his right temple and rebounded to Phil Sharpe at first slip who caught it. Close seemed none the worse – or at least would not admit it. When he returned to the pavilion at the next interval a member said to him. 'That was a terrible blow. You were standing dangerously close. What *would* have happened if the ball had hit you slap between the eyes?' Without hesitation the indomitable Yorkshire captain replied: 'He'd have been caught at cover.'

Patsy Hendren told many stories about himself, some of them I am sure apocryphal. Once when travelling in a train on his way to a match he said that he sat opposite an ashen-faced stranger, who had his collar turned up around his ears. He looked so ill and miserable that the kindly Patsy asked him what the trouble was. In a hoarse whisper – he was hardly able to speak – the man confided that he was a very keen cricketer but had recently let his side down badly. He had not only made five ducks in a row, but in the last match had dropped a vital catch off the last ball of the match. Had he caught it his side would have won. As it was, the opposition scored a run and won by one wicket. Said Patsy jokingly, trying to cheer the man up. 'Oh dear, oh dear, if I had done that I would have cut my throat.' The stranger replied hoarsely: 'I have.'

On another occasion Patsy was fielding on the boundary under the famous Hill at Sydney cricket ground. An Australian batsman hit the ball in the air towards him. As it soared higher and higher into the air, a raucous voice from the Hill shouted out: 'Patsy, if you miss that catch you can sleep with my sister.' Someone later asked Patsy what he had done. 'Oh,' he replied. 'As I hadn't seen his sister, I decided to catch the ball.'

When he was at school the irrascible TV personality Gilbert Harding hated cricket. He was fat, short-sighted and couldn't bat or field. His headmaster finally told him he could be excused playing cricket so long as he went for walks instead.

This infuriated the young games master. He thought it dreadful that someone should walk instead of playing cricket. So he thought he would get his own back on Gilbert, by making him act as umpire in the annual match of Masters *v.* The Boys. The Masters batted first and the young games master, resplendent in his Oxford University Authentic's Cap batted superbly and had reached 99 when a bowler from the end at which Gilbert was umpiring hit the games master high on his chest with a bouncer. The bowler tried to stifle his appeal for lbw, but not before Gilbert raised his finger and shouted 'out'. The games master was (quite rightly!) furious and as he passed Gilbert on the way back to the pavilion said angrily: 'Harding. You weren't paying attention. I wasn't out.' Gilbert thought for a second, then replied: 'On the contrary sir. I *was* paying attention. And you *weren't* out!'

A Kent amateur wicket-keeper used to enjoy his pints of beer at the end of a day's play. One morning he had a dreadful hang-over and entered the dressing room apparently in a trance. Kent were fielding so his colleagues helped him on with his pads, box and wicket-keeping gloves and 'steered' him out to the middle. They set him down about fifteen yards behind the stumps as the opening over was to be bowled by a young fast bowler. The first ball went 'whoosh' past the wicket-keeper's right ear. He never moved and the ball went for four byes. The second ball went past his left ear and still the wicket-keeper remained in a crouching position without moving. Another four byes were signalled. But the third ball was down the leg-side and the batsman, trying to glide it, just got an outside edge off his bat. The wicket-keeper took off and diving full length to his left, held a miraculous catch inches off the ground. He got up, tossed the ball in the air and walking across to the slips said: 'Do you know, gentleman. That's the first time I've ever caught a batsman off the *first* ball of the day!'

Appendices

Appendix 1:
Glossary of Terms and Equipment

APPEALS

If the fielding side believes that the batsman is out they appeal to the umpire with the call 'How's that?' This covers all ten ways of being out although the fielding side can be more specific, if they wish, and actually name the law i.e. 'How's that stumped?' In that case the umpire at square leg would say 'out' or 'not out', and the batsman could not be given out for anything else unless a new appeal was made. Although the ball is 'dead' on 'over' being called an appeal can still be made *before* the first ball of the next over is bowled. But no further appeal may be made after the umpires have removed the bails when time has been called either for close of play or for the lunch or tea intervals.

The captain of the fielding side may ask the umpire's permission to withdraw an appeal, providing the outgoing batsman has not left the playing area. If this withdrawal is allowed, the umpire shall cancel his decision.

BACKING UP

The non-striking batsman is said to be 'backing up' when he advances a few paces up the pitch after delivery of the ball, in expectation of a possible run. By so doing he makes it easier to 'steal' a short single. Backing up is also applied to the fielding side, when one fielder covers another in case he misses the ball. This is especially the case when the ball is returned to the wicket-keeper or bowler when the batsmen are running.

BACK STROKE

Usually made off a short-pitched ball. The batsman steps back with the weight on the right foot which is moved back and across in front of the stumps. It should be kept parallel to the popping crease (q.v.) while the batsman's body remains in as sideways on a position as possible.

BAILS

The two bails are each 4⅜ inches long and when in position in the grooves at the top of the stumps must not project more than ½ inch above them. The stumps and bails at each end of the pitch constitute the wicket, although the pitch (q.v.) is often wrongfully called the wicket.

BALL

The ball must not weigh less than 5½ nor more than 5¾ oz. The circumference must not be less than 8¹³/₁₆ inches nor more than 9 inches. It is made of red leather with an interior of cork bound with twine.

BAT

The bat must not exceed 4¼ inches in its widest part and shall not be more than 38 inches in length. There is no limit to its weight but the average bat varies from 2lb 4oz to 2lb 8oz with some players like Clive Lloyd, Ian Botham and Graham Gooch using bats up to 3lbs 4oz. The bat must be made of wood. The blade is made of willow and the handle of cane with thin strips of rubber in between. This is bound round with twine over which is placed a rubber grip.

BATTING-GLOVES

Worn on both hands to protect the fingers. Nowadays they are usually made of leather or cotton with a padding of stripped leather on the back of each finger and thumb. Should always be worn.

BEAMER

A full pitch bowled at a batsman's head, either intentionally or unintentionally.

BLOCK HOLE

The hole made by a batsman on or just behind the popping crease, when he marks the position of his guard given by the umpire.

BOSIE

The Australian name for the googly – after its inventor B J T Bosanquet.

BOUNCER

A short-pitched ball (see Bumper).

BOUNDARY
The outside limit of the playing area. Length is decided by the Home Authority with a maximum of 90 yards.

BOWLING CREASE
This crease is in line with the stumps and is 8 feet 8 inches in length with the stumps in the centre.

BOX
A triangular-shaped shield made of aluminium or plastic and, like batting-gloves, should always be worn. Some boxes can be strapped round the waist, but the easiest way is to wear a jock-strap and place the box inside it in a specially designed pouch.

BREAK-BACK
Another name for an off-break.

BUMP BALL
A ball which the batsman hits hard into the ground, so that when fielded by a fielder close to the wicket it gives the appearance of being a catch.

BUMPER
A short-pitched ball which rises sharply. The bowling of bumpers is unfair if, in the opinion of the umpire at the bowler's end, it constitutes an attempt to intimidate the striker. Umpires will consider intimidation to be the deliberate bowling of fast short-pitched balls which by their length, height and direction are intended to, or are likely to, injure the batsman. The same applies to fast high full pitches aimed at the batsman's head.

In the event of such unfair bowling the umpire at the bowler's end must:

a) In the first instance call and signal *no ball* and caution the bowler, at the same time informing the other umpire and the captain of the fielding side what has happened.
b) The next time the bowler bowls a ball which is considered unfair, the umpire must repeat the above procedure and tell the bowler that it is the final warning.
c) At the next repetition by the same bowler – no matter at which end the bowler is bowling, the umpire must again call and signal no ball, and when the ball is dead, direct the captain to take the bowler off forthwith and finish the over with another bowler. *The offending bowler may not then bowl again in the same innings.*

BYE

A run scored from a ball which passes the wicket without touching the bat or batsman and which the wicket-keeper fails to stop. If the ball touches any part of the batsman, except his hands, the runs are scored as leg-byes.

CARRY ONE'S BAT

If an opening batsman is still not out when the last wicket falls he is said to have 'carried his bat'.

CHAMPIONSHIP PENNANT

A flag to denote the holders of the County Championship. Instituted by Warwickshire in 1951, the pennant is given by the county holding the Championship to the winners in the following season. Warwickshire gave a pennant to Surrey at the end of the 1952 season, and after winning the Championship for seven years running, they in turn gave one to Yorkshire in 1959, and so on. The pennant shows the year of the Championship, the holder's badge in the centre, and the badges of the other sixteen counties round the edge. You will always see this pennant flying over the pavilion wherever last year's Champions are playing.

CHINAMAN

The left-arm bowler's off-break to a right-handed batsman.

CHOP

A form of late cut, made by bringing the bat down sharply on the ball just as it is about to pass the batsman on the off-side.

CLOSE OF PLAY

The time arranged for play to finish. In Test and County cricket there are now regulations stipulating that a certain number of overs *must* be bowled during the day. These tend to vary from year to year. But in 1985 for Test cricket it was 90 overs so that although the hours of play were 11 a.m. – 6 p.m., if by 6 p.m. the required 90 overs had not been bowled, then the game went on until they had been. Similarly in County cricket in 1985 the required number of overs was 112, so that although the official hours of play were 11 a.m. – 6.30 p.m. play had to go on until the 112 overs had been bowled.

Various rather complicated calculations are made for loss of time due to rain, bad light or an interval between innings. But basically in Test matches play is reduced by one over for every 4 minutes lost. In County cricket it was one over for every 3½ minutes lost.

In both Test and County cricket when one hour of the official hours of play remains on the *last* day a minimum of 20 overs must be bowled in that final hour. If they are completed *before* the time for Close of Play then play must continue until the official time is up. But if at that time the 20 overs have not yet been completed then play must go on until they have been. The only exceptions to this are:

1. If the match is finished.

2. If with half an hour left *both* captains agree to call the match off.

N.B. – An over in progress at the advertised time for Close of Play on the *final* day of a match must be completed, at the request of either captain, even if a wicket falls after 'time' has been reached.

COW-SHOT
A swipe across the flight of a ball from off to leg which sends the ball anywhere on the leg side.

CROSS-BAT
A stroke made with the bat when out of the true perpendicular; similar in principle to the 'cow-shot'.

DEAD BALL
The ball becomes dead when:

1. It is finally settled in the hands of the wicket-keeper or the bowler.

2. It reaches, or pitches over, the boundary.

3. A batsman is out.

4. Whether played or not, it lodges in the clothing or equipment of a batsman or the clothing of an umpire.

5. A ball lodges in a protective helmet worn by a member of the fielding side.

6. A penalty is awarded under Law 20 (Lost Ball) or Law 41.1 (Fielding the Ball).

7. The umpire calls 'over' or 'time'.

Either umpire must call the signal 'Dead Ball' when:

1. He intervenes in a case of unfair play.

2. A serious injury to a player or umpire occurs.

3. He is satisfied that, for an adequate reason, the batsman is not ready to receive the ball and makes no attempt to play it.

4. The bowler drops the ball accidentally before delivery or the ball does not leave his hand for any reason.

5. One or both bails fall from the batsman's wicket before he receives the delivery.

6. He, the umpire, leaves his normal position for consultation.

7. He is required to do so under Law 26.3 (Disallowance of leg-byes when the batsman has not attempted a stroke).

The ball ceases to be Dead when the Bowler starts his run up or bowling action.

N.B. – The ball is *not* DEAD when:

1. It strikes an umpire (unless it lodges in his clothing).

2. The wicket is broken or struck down (unless a batsman is out – stumped, run out, or hit wicket).

3. An unsuccessful appeal is made.

4. The wicket is broken accidentally either by the bowler during his delivery or by a batsman in running.

5. The umpire has called 'no ball' or 'wide'.

DECLARATION OF AN INNINGS
The captain of the batting side may declare an innings closed at any time during a match irrespective of its duration.

A captain may forfeit his second innings provided his decision to do so is notified to the opposing captain and umpires in sufficient time to allow 7 minutes rolling of the pitch. The normal 10 minutes interval between innings must be applied.

DONKEY DROP
A ball bowled very high in the air.

DRAW
An undecided match. Also used to describe an old-fashioned stroke, where the batsman cocked his left leg up and deflected the ball underneath – down towards long-leg.

DRINKS ON THE FIELD
Drinks can only be taken to the same team in the field *once* in each session.

DUCK
The dreaded score of 0.

EXTRAS
Runs added to the score but not actually scored by the batsman. They consist of byes, leg-byes, wides and no-balls. As from 1985 no balls and wides are debited to the bowler concerned, so affecting his final analysis.

FLIGHT
The term used for a ball so delivered that in its passage through the air it deceives the batsman as to the spot where it will touch the ground. Spin aids flight as the ball is inclined to dip just before hitting the ground.

FLIPPER
A type of delivery which is said to have been invented by Clarrie Grimmett and also bowled by Bruce Dooland, Richie Benaud, Bob Barber, and even by Ken Barrington. It is a ball held in the tips of the first and third fingers of the right hand. It is squeezed or flipped out of the hand from underneath the wrist – rather like flipping a cherry stone. Pitched outside the off stump it hurries through off the pitch, usually straight but sometimes from off to leg. A very useful surprise weapon if bowled occasionally, especially at a batsman who tends to play off the back foot or one who likes the pull shot off slow bowlers.

FOLLOW-ON
The side which bats first and leads by 200 runs in a match of more than four days, by 150 runs in a match of four or three days, by 100 runs in a two-day match, or by 75 runs on a one-day match, has the option of asking the other side to follow-on i.e. to bat again immediately.

FULL TOSS OR FULL PITCH
A ball which reaches the batsman at the popping-crease without pitching. A ball can be made into a full toss by a batsman advancing down the pitch and hitting the ball before it touches the ground.

GOOGLY

A ball bowled out of the back of the right hand with what looks like a leg-break action, but which spins as an off-break when hitting the ground and so turns 'the wrong way', contrary to the batsman's expectations.

GO AWAY

A ball which leaves a batsman, i.e. moves from leg to off either in the air or off the pitch, is said to 'go away'.

GO WITH THE ARM

A term for a ball which appears to go with the direction of the bowler's arm, i.e. for a right-arm bowler it is, in fact, a continuation of an out-swinger, and for a left-arm bowler, the continuation of an in-swinger, when both are bowling to a right-handed batsman.

GREEN WICKET

A pitch well covered with plenty of grass which early in the day contains quite a lot of moisture. This is sometimes caused because the pitch has been covered all night and has 'sweated'. The greenness helps the pace bowler to get extra life and movement off the pitch.

GRUB

A ball which shoots along the ground. Also called a 'sneak'.

GUARD

Given to the batsman by the umpire at the bowler's end, so that the batsman knows the position of his bat and feet in relation to the three stumps which he is guarding. Guard is given from behind the bowler's wicket unless otherwise asked for. The usual guards are: middle, middle and leg, or leg stump.

HALF VOLLEY

A ball which the bat strikes just after the ball leaves the ground.

HANDLED BALL

Either batsman may be dismissed 'handled ball' if he touches the ball, while in play, with his hands, unless he does so at the request of the fielding side.

HAT TRICK

The feat of a bowler taking three wickets with three consecutive deliveries either in one over or spread over two overs. By longstanding custom three wickets in three balls spread over two innings of the same match is regarded as a 'hat trick', but the limit ends there and three wickets in three balls spread over two matches do not qualify for a 'hat trick'.

HOOK

A stroke to leg off a short rising ball, pitched usually on the wicket or leg-side.

IN-SWINGER

A ball which swings from off to leg in flight, thus moving into the batsman while still in the air.

KING PAIR

If a batsman is out first ball for 0 in each innings, he is said to have made a 'king pair'.

LAP

An expression used by modern cricketers to describe a cross-bat stroke. The batsman hits across the flight of the ball and even though it pitches on or outside the off stump, he hits it somewhere between square-leg and mid-on.

LAST OVER

The last over before an interval or close of play will be started provided that the umpire, after walking at his normal pace, has arrived at his position behind the stumps at the bowler's end.

The last over before an interval or close of play will be completed unless a batsman is out or retires during that over within 2 minutes of the interval or close of play.

An over in progress at the time for close of play on the *final* day of a match will be completed at the request of either captain even if a wicket falls after time has been reached. But if during the last over the players leave the field for rain or bad light the umpire will immediately call time and there will be no resumption of play, and the match will have ended.

LATE CUT

A stroke played to a short ball outside the off stump by stepping across with the right foot and hitting the ball down with a wristy action, so sending it past the slips.

LEG-BREAK

A ball which turns on the pitch from the leg-side to the off. The orthodox spin for a left arm bowler is a leg-break to a right-handed batsman.

LEG-BYES

If the ball, not having been called 'wide' or 'no ball' is *unintentionally* deflected by the batsman's dress or person – except a hand holding the bat – and any runs are obtained the umpire will signal leg-bye and the run or runs will be credited to the batting side. Such leg-byes shall only be scored if, in the opinion of the umpire, the batsman has:

1. Attempted to play the ball with his bat.

2. Tried to avoid being hit by the ball.

Deliberate deflection with the body is unfair and the umpire will call Dead Ball as soon as he is satisfied that the fielding side has no chance of dismissing either batsman.

LEG-CUTTER

A fast leg-break which is bowled by 'cutting' across the seam of the ball rather than using the normal wrist-spin.

LEG-SIDE

The side of the pitch behind the batsman as he takes his stand at the wicket. The number of fielders on the leg-side behind the popping crease must not exceed two at the instant of the bowler's delivery. If there are more than two the square-leg umpire must call 'No-ball'. There is no limit to the number of fielders allowed on the leg-side as a whole.

LEG-TRAP

A term used to describe a cluster of fielders in the short-leg positions.

LENGTH

A good-length ball is one which pitches on the pitch at such a distance from the batsman as to make him uncertain whether to play a backward or forward stroke. It is a ball which he cannot reach comfortably by playing forward, or adequately deal with by playing back, as the ball is too far up for the latter type of stroke.

LOB
A method of bowling which is rarely seen in first-class cricket today. Bowled under-arm, it is a survivor of the earliest known form of bowling. If the ball is returned under-arm by the fielder he is said to 'lob' it. The lob is no longer allowed in limited-over cricket.

LONG-FIELD
The part of the outfield in front of the sight-screen in the region of long-off and long-on.

LONG HANDLE
The aggressive batsman who is hitting out is sometimes said to be 'using the long handle'.

LONG HOP
A very short-pitched ball.

MAIDEN OVER
An over off which no runs are scored by the batsmen. Also, since 1985, one in which no no-balls or wides are bowled, since these are now debited in the bowler's analysis.

MIDDLE
The centre of the ground or the square upon which the pitches are prepared.

NEW BALL
Either captain can demand a new ball at the start of each innings. The captain of the fielding side has the option of taking another new ball after:

1. 85 overs in Test matches.

2. 100 overs in other matches.

The taking of the new ball can be delayed, but the counting of overs for another new ball does not start until the new ball has been taken (i.e. if a Test captain delays taking a new ball until 100 overs have been bowled, another new one is not due until after the 185th over.

NIGHT-WATCHMAN

A lower-order batsman sent in to play out time when a wicket falls shortly before close of play. This saves the risk of a better batsman losing his wicket – often in failing light.

NO-BALL

For a delivery to be fair, the ball must be bowled, not thrown. If either umpire be not entirely satisfied of the absolute fairness of a delivery in this respect, he shall call and signal 'No-ball' instantly upon delivery. The umpire at the bowler's wicket shall call and signal 'No ball' if, in the delivery stride no part of the bowler's front foot is behind the popping crease, whether grounded or raised, or if he is not satisfied that the bowler's back foot has landed within (but not touching) the return crease or its forward extension.

A ball shall be deemed to have been thrown if, in the opinion of either umpire the process of straightening the bowling arm, whether it be partial or complete, takes place during that part of the delivery swing which directly precedes the ball leaving the hand. This definition shall not debar a bowler from the use of the wrist in the delivery swing.

In conjunction with the above-mentioned experimental law the following conditions shall apply:

1. The length of the return crease shall be 4 feet.

2. The popping crease shall extend 6 feet either side of the line of stumps.

3. The popping crease and return crease shall be re-drawn during each interval.

The umpire will also call 'No ball':

1. If the bowler fails to notify the batsman that he is changing his delivery, i.e. from over the wicket to round the wicket, from over-arm to lobs, etc.

2. If there are more than two fielders behind the popping crease on the leg-side.

3. If a bowler, before delivery, throws the ball at the striker's wicket even in an attempt to run him out.

The following points are also important:

1. A batsman may be out in four ways off 'No-ball': Run out, handling the ball, obstructing the field, hitting the ball twice.

2. The ball does not become dead upon the call 'No ball', and if runs are scored by the batsman they are credited to the score and debited to the bowler. If no runs are scored, then one 'No ball' is added to the extras.

3. Any byes or leg-byes made off a 'No ball' are scored as 'No balls'.

4. A 'No ball' does *not* count in the over so an extra ball has to be bowled for every 'No ball' bowled, in order that the 'Over' may consist of six legitimate deliveries.

5. The umpire signals 'No ball' by extending one arm horizontally.

N.B.

1. In limited over cricket it is now a 'no ball' if there are fewer than four fielders within the 30 yard circle at the point of delivery.

2. Since 1985, no-balls and wides have been debited against the bowler's analysis though still counting as extras in the score.

OFF-BREAK
A ball which after pitching turns from off to leg. Bowled by a right-arm bowler, it is referred to as orthodox spin. Spun mainly by the first finger of the right hand, the action is like turning a door handle.

OFF-CUTTER
A fast off-break bowled by 'cutting' across the seam of the ball rather than by orthodox finger spin.

OFF-DRIVE
A drive made off the front foot, usually from a half-volley, in the arc between cover-point and long off.

OFF SIDE
The side of the field 'in front' of the batsman as he takes his stand at the wicket.

ON-DRIVE
A drive made off the front foot in the arc between mid-wicket and long-on.

ON SIDE
The same as leg-side, i.e. the side of the field behind the batsman.

OUTFIELD
That portion of the playing area which is some distance from the pitch. The fielding positions are nearer the boundary than the pitch (e.g. long-off, long-on, deep third man, long-leg, deep mid-wicket, etc.).

OVER
An 'over' of six balls is bowled from each end alternately. Australia, New Zealand and South Africa have at various times had eight ball overs and here in England the eight ball over was tried in County cricket during the 1939 season.

OUT OF HIS GROUND
The batsman must have some part of his bat or his foot on the ground behind the popping crease in order to avoid being run out or stumped. If he does not he is held to be 'Out of his ground'. The foot positioned on the line is 'Out'. It is not enough for a batsman to have foot or the bat in the air behind the crease, *it must be grounded*.

OUT-SWINGER
A ball which swings from leg to off in flight, often described as 'leaving the bat'.

OVER THE WICKET
A term used to describe from which side of the stumps a bowler is bowling. A right-arm bowler delivers the ball from the left hand-side, a left-arm bowler from the right.

OVERTHROW
A throw in from the field which eludes the wicket-keeper or bowler and travels beyond the stumps to the other side of the field, so that the batsmen may take further runs. If a ball hits the stumps with a batsman in his crease, and then ricochets off to the outfield, over-throws may still be taken even though the wicket is broken. All such runs scored are credited to the striker and (rather bad luck this) debited to the bowler, unless of course they are extras to start with.

PAIR OF SPECTACLES
A term used to describe the performance of a batsman who fails to score in both innings of a match, thereby collecting two 'ducks'.

PAYMENT OF PLAYERS AND UMPIRES IN TEST MATCHES

Players are paid £1,500 per Test for each of their first ten Tests. This is increased by £50 per Test after every subsequent ten Tests.

Umpires receive £1,300 per Test.

PITCH

A playing area 22 yards long and 5 feet in width on either side of a line joining the two middle stumps. A pitch may not be changed *during* a match unless it becomes unfit for play, and then only with the consent of *both* captains.

PLAYED ON

A colloquial term used for a batsman who is dismissed 'Bowled' through hitting the ball into his own wicket with the bat.

PLAYING BACK

A stroke played by the batsman with his weight on the back foot, i.e. the foot nearest the stumps and the right foot in the case of a right-handed batsman. This stroke is usually used when playing a ball which is short of a length.

PLUMB PITCH OR WICKET

A perfect surface which has not been affected by either rain or wear. It gives no help to swing or spin bowlers as the ball comes off at a uniform height and pace, without any real change of direction. Ideal for batting.

POLISHING THE BALL

Any member of the fielding side may polish the ball provided that such polishing wastes no time, and that no artificial substance is used. No one may rub the ball on the ground nor use any artificial substance nor take any other action to alter the condition of the ball. For instance a player may not lift the seam of the ball for any reason. If he does the umpire will immediately change the ball for one of similar condition to that in use before the lifting.

POP

A ball which lifts sharply off the pitch is said to 'Pop'.

POPPING CREASE
A line 4 feet in front of the wicket parallel to the bowling crease. It is the forward limit of the batsman's safety area against stumping and run-out decisions.

PULL
A stroke made by hitting across the flight of a ball delivered on the stumps or off-side of the wicket and driving it away to the on-side. This is technically a forward stroke off the front foot. The bat remains perpendicular throughout as distinct from the cow-shot.

QUALIFICATION REGULATIONS
These are far too complicated to list in full. It would take a book in itself. But briefly for a cricketer to qualify for England:

1. He must have been born in the British Isles.

OR

2. His father or mother must have been born in the British Isles and he himself have resided in the British Isles for the previous four consecutive years. But if he has played first-class cricket in the country of his origin, the four year period must be increased by one year for each season he played – up to a maximum of ten years.

OR

3. He must have resided in the British Isles for the previous ten consecutive years and not have played in a Test or International for any other country during that period.

OR

4. He must have been resident in the British Isles both for the previous four consecutive years, and since the day before his fourteenth birthday, and not have played for any other country during those periods.

A cricketer is qualified to play for a county if it is:

1. The county of his birth.

OR

2. The county in which he is residing and has been resident for the previous twelve consecutive months.

OR

3. The county for which his father played regularly.

N.B. – No county may play more than one cricketer *not qualified to play for England*. But they may register more than one if they so wish. This does not apply to an overseas cricketer registered for a county on 28 November 1978 or if bonafide negotiations had been begun *before* that date and completed before the start of the 1979 season.

RETIREMENTS
A batsman may retire at any time but cannot resume his innings without the consent of the fielding captain and then only *at the fall of a wicket*. A batsman is regarded as 'Not out' if he retires as a result of injury or illness but it counts as 'Out' if he retires for any other reason.

RETURN CREASE
A line which turns back at right angles at each end of the bowling crease and is deemed to be of unlimited length. Since the introduction of the front foot law for calling 'No-balls', the return crease is extended from the bowling crease to the popping crease.

ROLLING, MOWING, AND WATERING
1. The pitch cannot be rolled during a match except before the start of each innings and of each day's play, when, if the captain of the batting side chooses, it can be swept and rolled for *not more than 7 minutes*. It can be rolled for less if the captain so wishes. Rolling before play must take place not *more* than 30 minutes before play is due to start, and the captain of the batting side can delay this rolling until ten minutes before the start if he wishes. But if the captain of the batting side only declares his innings closed just before the start, the time for sufficient rolling must be taken out of the normal playing period, if necessary. This also applies if a declaration is made later than 15 minutes after the start of the lunch interval. Play will then not restart until 2.20 p.m.

2. In a match for two or more days duration the pitch shall be mown daily before play begins.

3. If conditions permit the outfield will be mown before the start of play on each morning of the match. The pitch *cannot* be watered in any circumstances during a match.

ROUND THE WICKET
To bowl round the wicket a right-arm bowler delivers the ball from the right-hand side of the stumps, and a left-arm bowler from the left-hand side.

RUNNER

A runner is allowed for a batsman who *during the match* is incapacitated by injury or illness. The player acting as the runner must be a member of the batting side, and, if possible, should already have batted in that innings. He must also wear gloves and pads if the injured batsman is so equipped.

The injured batsman is out if his runner handles the ball, obstructs the field or is run out. The injured batsman can also be out stumped or run out whilst at the striker's end, but when he is the non-striker he is out of the game and must stand out of the way alongside the square leg umpire.

RUN-UP

To cut out time-wasting the bowler is not now allowed a trial run-up after 'Play' has been called in any session, except at the fall of a wicket and then only if it will not cause any waste of time.

SEAM BOWLER OR SEAMER

A bowler – normally of medium pace or faster – who 'moves' the ball in the air or off the pitch.

SESSION

A session is one of the three official periods of play, i.e. from start to lunch, from lunch to tea, from tea to close of play.

SET

A batsman is said to be 'Set' when he has got his 'eye in' or has 'played himself in'.

SHINE

'Shine on the ball' means that it still retains some of the smooth polished surface which it had when new. A smooth surface helps the ball to swing, which is why you see seam bowlers polishing the ball (q.v.).

SHOOTER

A ball which does not rise after hitting the ground. Also referred to as a 'squatter'.

SHORT RUN

When a batsman fails to make good his ground at one end when running two or more runs. The umpire signals this, and the scorers delete one or more runs from those actually run by the batsmen.

SHOULDER ARMS

An expression used to describe a batsman's action when he holds the bat aloft over his shoulder as he allows the ball to go by on the off-side without attempting a stroke.

SIGHT-SCREEN

In Test matches in this country sight-screens must now be provided at both ends of the ground.

SQUARE CUT

A stroke made to a short ball outside the off stump by stepping across the wicket and hitting the ball down with a wristy action as it is level with the batsman. This stroke will normally send the ball between cover point and gully down towards third man.

START OF PLAY

This varies, but in Test matches in this country and also in the County Championship the start is at 11.00 a.m.

STUMPS

Must be of equal size and placed into the ground so that the ball cannot pass between them. When in position the three stumps together are 9 inches wide, each stump being 28 inches above the ground.

SUBSTITUTES

No player may leave the field or return during a session without the consent of the umpire at the bowler's end.

Substitutes are allowed by right to field for any player who *during the match* is incapacitated by illness or injury. The consent of the opposing captain must be obtained for the use of a substitute if any player is prevented from fielding for any other reason. The opposing captain cannot object to any player acting as substitute in the field, nor as to where he may field, with the exception of the position of wicket-keeper.

If a player wishes to change his shirt, boots, etc he may leave the field to do so on getting permission from the umpire at the bowler's end. But no substitute is allowed to replace him.

N.B.

1. A substitute may *not* bat or bowl.

2. If a member of the fielding side does not take the field at the start of play, leaves the field or fails to return after an interval and is absent from the field for longer than 15 minutes:

a) He may not bowl on that day after his return until he has been on the field for at least the length of playing time for which he was absent.

b) He may not bat on that day unless or until, in the aggregate, he has returned to the field and/or his side's innings has been in progress for at least the length of time for which he has been absent. Or, if earlier, when his side has lost five wickets.

SWEEP

A stroke played with a horizontal bat at a ball which is usually on or outside the leg stump. The bat follows round and hits the ball behind the wicket on the leg-side, down towards long leg or fine leg.

TAIL

The players engaged more for their bowling or wicket-keeping abilities than for their prowess as batsmen and who are not expected to score many runs are known as the 'Tail' or 'Tail-enders'. They are also sometimes referred to as 'Rabbits.' One player was so notoriously bad as a batsman that he gained the nickname of 'Ferret' – the man who comes in after the 'Rabbits'.

TEA INTERVAL

The regulations governing this are the nightmare of the commentators, spectators and even umpires. Basically they are as given on pages 30–39.

TEAM

A first-class match is played between two teams of eleven players each. Before tossing for choice of innings the two captains must exchange lists of their teams in writing, together with the twelfth man. Afterwards no alteration can be made in either team without the consent of the opposing captain. In practice this will probably be given in the event of sudden illness or injury before the match starts.

TIE

A match which ends with an equal total of runs scored by each side, provided that the fourth innings is completed.

TIME WASTING

Any form of time wasting is unfair. An umpire may warn a captain who is wasting time, and after three warnings must report him to the captain of the batting side and to the executive of the fielding side.

A bowler taking an unnecessarily long time to bowl an over can be warned twice by the umpire and if he then repeats the offence can be taken off immediately by the umpire for the rest of the innings.

TOP SPIN

Spin which allows the ball to gain pace off the pitch when hitting the ground and then to continue on the same line. Bowled by leg-break bowlers in addition to the googly.

TOSS FOR INNINGS

The choice of innings is by the toss of a coin. The home captain tosses the coin, the visiting captain calls. The toss must be made not later than 15 minutes before the scheduled time for the match to start, or in the case of a delayed start, 15 minutes before the time agreed upon to start. Before they toss the captains must exchange the names of their eleven chosen players in writing.

TRACK

A slang expression for the pitch. A batsman is sometimes said to 'go down the track' to a slow bowler.

UMPIRES

Two umpires are appointed and cannot be changed during a match without the consent of both captains. Before the toss for innings they must agree with the captains any special regulations and all conditions affecting the match i.e. hours of play, intervals, which clock they are going by, choice of balls to be used and any local rules affecting the boundary.

They must also see that the wickets are properly pitched and that all playing equipment such as bats, balls and stumps conform to the laws.

An umpire may alter his decision provided he does so promptly. He must also intervene if a batsman, not having been given out, has left his wicket under a misapprehension. The various umpires' signals are shown on pages 206 and 207.

WICKET-KEEPER

A wicket-keeper must remain wholly behind the wicket until a ball delivered by the bowler touches the bat or person of the batsman or

Bye: by raising the open
                 hand above the head.

Leg-bye: by touching a raised
                 knee with the hand.

One short: by touching the
                shoulder with the tips
                of the fingers.

Wide: by extending both
                arms horizontally.

No-ball: by extending one arm horizontally.

Out: by raising the index finger.

Six: by raising both hands above the head.

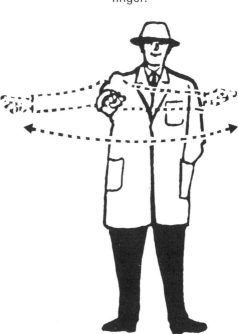

Four: by waving the outstretched hand from side to side.

passes the wicket, or until the batsman attempts a run. If the wicket-keeper contravenes this law the umpire at the batsman's end must call and signal No Ball at the instant of delivery or as soon as possible afterwards.

The wicket-keeper can 'stump' the batsman if the latter, in receiving a ball – not being a no ball – is out of his ground other than in attempting a run. In that case the batsman would be run out. To stump a batsman the wicket-keeper must break the wicket with the ball in his hands, or in one hand provided that is the hand that breaks the wicket.

The wicket-keeper must always take the ball *behind* the wicket, except if it has touched the bat or person of the batsman. In that case the wicket-keeper may stump a batsman from *in front* of the wicket. It is also out stumped if the ball is thrown by the wicket-keeper or if it rebounds off his pads.

WICKET MAIDEN
An over off which no runs no balls or wides are scored but in which the bowler takes one or more wickets.

WIDE BALL
The ball is called a wide by the umpire at the bowler's end if it is bowled so high over, or wide of the wicket that in the umpire's opinion the ball is out of the reach of a batsman when taking guard *in the normal position*.

N.B.

a) A batsman can be stumped off a wide.

b) If a wide goes past the wicket-keeper to the boundary it counts as 4 wides, NOT 4 byes.

WISDEN TROPHY
A trophy which is played for by England and the West Indies. Presented by Wisden to celebrate their centenary.

WRONG-UN
Another term used to denote the googly, called a 'Bosie' in Australia after B J T Bosanquet, the originator.

YORKER
A ball well pitched up so that it touches the ground at the batsman's feet and is liable to pass under the bat. A very useful ball for a pace bowler to bowl at a new batsman.

Appendix 2: Main Cricket Records

Compiled by Bill Frindall

All records are complete to the end of the 1985 English season. The Test records include official Test Matches only.

* denotes a not-out innings or an unfinished partnership.

A. ALL FIRST-CLASS CRICKET

1. Team Records

Highest Innings Total
    1,107   Victoria *v.* New South Wales (Melbourne) 1926–27
Highest Second Innings Total
    770   New South Wales *v.* South Australia (Adelaide) 1920–21
Highest Fourth Innings Total
    654 for 5 (set 696)   England *v.* South Africa (Durban) 1938–39
Highest Match Aggregate
    2,376 (for 38 wkts)   Bombay *v.* Maharashtra (Poona) 1948–49
Largest Margin of Victory
    Innings and 851 runs: Railways *v.* Dera Ismail Khan (Lahore) 1964–65
Victory Without Losing a Wicket
    Lancashire beat Leicestershire by 10 wkts (Manchester) 1956
    Karachi A beat Sind A by an innings and 77 runs (Karachi) 1957–58
    Railways beat Jammu and Kashmir by 10 wickets (Srinagar) 1960–61
    Karnataka beat Kerala by an innings and 186 runs (Chikmagalur) 1977–78
Most Runs in a Day
    721   Australians *v.* Essex (Southend) 1948
Lowest Innings Total
    12   Oxford University *v.* MCC (Oxford) 1877
    12   Northamptonshire *v.* Gloucestershire (Gloucester) 1907
Lowest Match Aggregate by One Team
    34   Border (16 and 18) *v.* Natal (East London) 1959–60
Lowest Match Aggregate – Both Teams in Completed Match
    105 (for 31 wkts)   MCC *v.* Australians (Lord's) 1878
Fewest Runs in an Uninterrupted Day's Play
    95   Australians (80) *v.* Pakistan (15 for 2) at Karachi 1956–57
Teams Scoring Most Centuries in an Innings
    6   Holkar (912 for 8 dec.) *v.* Mysore (Indore) 1945–46

2. Players' Records (Individual Batting)

Highest Individual Innings
499   Hanif Mohammad: Karachi *v.* Bahawalpur (Karachi) 1958–59

Most Hundreds in Successive Innings
6   C B Fry for Sussex and Rest of England 1901
6   D G Bradman for South Australia and Bradman's XI 1938–39
6   M J Procter for Rhodesia 1970–71

Most Hundreds in a Season
18   D C S Compton for England, Middlesex and the South 1947

Two Double-Centuries in a Match
A E Fagg (244 and 202★)   Kent *v.* Essex (Colchester) 1938

Double Century and Century in a Match Most Times
4   Zaheer Abbas (Gloucestershire)

Two Separate Centuries in an Innings Most Times
8   Zaheer Abbas (Gloucestershire and PIA)

Most Hundreds in a Career
197   J B Hobbs (Surrey) 1905–34

Highest Score on Debut
240   W F E Marx: Transvaal *v.* Griqualand West (Johannesburg) 1920–21

Highest Maiden Hundred
337★   Pervez Akhtar: Railways *v.* Dera Ismail Khan (Lahore) 1964–65

Hundreds in First Three Innings in First-class Cricket
J S Solomon (114★, 108, 121) for British Guiana in 1956–57 and 1957–58

Most Runs in a Month
1,294   (Avge 92.42): L. Hutton (Yorkshire)................................... June 1949

Most Runs in a Season
3,816 (Avge 90.85): D C S Compton (Middlesex) 1947

Thousand Runs in a Season Most Times
28   W G Grace (Gloucestershire) and F E Woolley (Kent)

Earliest Dates for Scoring 1,000, 2,000 and 3,000 Runs in a Season
1,000 runs: May 27th (1938) – D G Bradman (Australians)
2,000 runs: July 5th (1906) – T W Hayward (Surrey)
3,000 runs: August 20th (1906) – T W Hayward (Surrey)
            August 20th (1937) W R Hammond (Gloucestershire)

Most Runs in a Career
61,237 (Avge 50.65): J B Hobbs (Surrey) 1905–34

Carrying Bat Through *both* Innings of a Match
H Jupp 43★ 109★   Surrey *v.* Yorkshire (Oval) 1874
S P Kinneir 70★ 69★   Warwickshire *v.* Leicestershire (Leicester) 1907
C J B Wood 107★ 117★   Leicestershire *v.* Yorkshire (Bradford) 1911
V M Merchant 135★ 77★   Indians *v.* Lancashire (Liverpool) 1936

Fast Scoring
Fastest 50: 8 min   C C Inman: Leicestershire *v.* Nottinghamshire
   (Nottingham) 1965
Fastest 100: 35 min   P G H Fender: Surrey *v.* Northamptonshire
   (Northampton) 1920
            35 min   S J O'Shaughnessy: Lancashire *v.* Leicestershire
   (Manchester)... 1983
Fastest 200: 113 min   R J Shastri: Bombay *v.* Baroda (Bombay)................. 1984–85
Fastest 300: 181 min   D C S Compton: MCC *v.* North-Eastern Transvaal
   (Benoni)... 1948–49

Most Runs in a Day
345   C G Macartney: Australians *v.* Nottinghamshire (Nottingham) 1921

Most Runs Off One Over
36   (666666) G St A Sobers off M A Nash: Nottinghamshire *v.* Glamorgan
   (Swansea) 1968

36   (666666) R J Shastri off Tilak Raj Bombay *v*. Baroda (Bombay).............. 1984–85
Most sixes in an Innings
15   J R Reid: Wellington *v*. Northern Districts (Wellington) 1962–63
Most Sixes in a Match
17   W J Stewart: Warwickshire *v*. Lancashire (Blackpool) 1959
Most Sixes in a Season
80   I T Botham (Somerset) 1985
Most Boundaries in an Innings
68   (all fours) P A Perrin: Essex *v*. Derbyshire (Chesterfield) 1904
Slow Scoring
Slowest 50: 361 min   T E Bailey: England *v*. Australia (Brisbane).............. 1958–59
Slowest 100: 557 min   Mudassar Nazar: Pakistan *v*. England (Lahore)......... 1977–78
Slowest 200: 652 min   A D Gaekwad: India *v*. Pakistan (Jullundur).............. 1983–84
Slowest 300: 858 min   Hanif Mohammad: Pakistan *v*. West Indies
(Bridgetown)... 1957–58
Longest Time Before Scoring First Run
97 min   T G Evans (10★): England *v*. Australia (Adelaide)......................... 1946–47
Longest Individual Innings
970 min   Hanif Mohammad (337): Pakistan *v*. West Indies (Bridgetown)....... 1957–58
Lowest Innings Totals to Include Individual Milestones
50: 66   (S Nazir Ali 52) Indians *v*. Yorkshire (Harrogate)....................... 1932
100: 143   (C E B Rice 105★) Nottinghamshire *v*. Hampshire (Bournemouth)... 1981
200: 298   (T W Graveney 200) Gloucestershire *v*. Glamorgan (Newport)........ 1956
300: 387   (V S Hazare 309) Rest *v*. Hindus (Bombay).............................. 1943–44
400: 793   (W H Ponsford 437) Victoria *v*. Queensland (Melbourne).............. 1927–28
Highest Percentage of Total
83.4   G M Turner (141★): Worcestershire (169) *v*. Glamorgan (Swansea) 1977
Most Innings Without Scoring
10   B J Griffiths (Northamptonshire).. 1974–77

3. Players' Records (Batting Partnerships)

World Record for Each Wicket
1st 561   Waheed Mirza and Mansoor Akhtar: Karachi Whites *v*. Quetta
         (Karachi) 1976–77
2nd 465★   J A Jameson and R B Kanhai: Warwickshire *v*. Gloucestershire
         (Birmingham) 1974
3rd 456   Khalid Irtiza and Aslam Ali: United Bank *v*. Multan (Karachi) 1975–76
4th 577   V S Hazare and Gul Mahomed: Baroda *v*. Holkar (Baroda) 1946–47
5th 405   S G Barnes and D G Bradman: Australia *v*. England (Sydney)........ 1946–47
6th 487★   G A Headley and C C Passailaigue: Jamaica *v*. Lord Tennyson's XI
         (Kingston) 1931–32
7th 347   D St E Atkinson and C C Depeiza: West Indies *v*. Australia
         (Bridgetown) 1954–55
8th 433   A Sims and V T Trumper: Australian XI *v*. Canterbury
         (Christchurch) 1913–14
9th 283   A Warren and J Chapman: Derbyshire *v*. Warwickshire (Blackwell)   1910
10th 307   A F Kippax and J E H Hooker: New South Wales *v*. Victoria
         (Melbourne) 1928–29

4. Players' Records (Bowling)

All Ten Wickets in an Innings at Least Cost
10 for 10   H Verity: Yorkshire *v*. Nottinghamshire (Leeds)....................... 1932
All Ten Wickets in an Innings on Most Occasions
3   A P Freeman:
10 for 131   Kent *v*. Lancashire (Maidstone) 1929

| 10 for 53 | Kent v. Essex (Southend) | 1930 |
| 10 for 79 | Kent v. Lancashire (Manchester) | 1931 |

Most Wickets in a Match
19 J C Laker (9 for 37 and 10 for 53): England v. Australia (Manchester) 1956

Most Wickets in Debut Match
15 J H Kirwan: Cambridge U v. Cambridge Town (Cambridge) 1836
15 W Brown: Tasmania v. Victoria (Hobart) 1857–58
15 Nadeem Malik: Lahore Reds v. Sargodha (Lahore) 1973–74

Most Wickets in a Day
17 C Blythe: Kent v. Northamptonshire (Northampton) 1907
17 H Verity: Yorkshire v. Essex (Leyton) 1933
17 T W Goddard: Gloucestershire v. Kent (Bristol) 1939

Most Wickets in a Season
304 (Avge 18.05) A P Freeman (Kent) 1928

Hundred Wickets in a Season Most Times
23 W Rhodes (Yorkshire)

Earliest Dates for Taking 100, 200, and 300 wickets in a Season
100 wickets: June 12th (1896) – J T Hearne (Middlesex)
             June 12th (1931) – C W L Parker (Gloucestershire)
200 wickets: July 27th (1928) – A P Freeman (Kent)
300 wickets: September 15th (1928) – A P Freeman (Kent)

Most Wickets in a Career
4,187 (Avge 16.70) W Rhodes (Yorkshire) 1898–1930

Four Wickets with Consecutive Balls (since 1946)
F Ridgway: Kent v. Derbyshire (Folkestone) 1951
A K Walker: Nottinghamshire v. Leicestershire (Leicester) 1956
S N Mohol: Board President's XI v. Combined XI (Poona) 1965–66
P I Pocock: Surrey v. Sussex (Eastbourne) 1972

Most Hat-Tricks in a Career
7 D V P Wright (Kent)

Performing Hat-Trick Twice in Same Innings
A E Trott: Middlesex v. Somerset (Lord's) 1907
J S Rao: Services v. Northern Punjab (Amritsar) 1963–64

Most Runs Conceded in an Innings
362 A A Mailey (64–0–362–4): New South Wales v. Victoria (Melbourne) 1926–27

Most Runs Conceded in a Match
428 C S Nayudu (6 for 153 and 5 for 275): Holkar v. Bombay (Bombay) 1944–45

Most Balls Bowled in an Innings
588 S Ramadhin (98–35–179–2): West Indies v. England (Birmingham) 1957

Most Balls Bowled in a Match
917 C S Nayudu (152.5–25–428–11): Holkar v. Bombay (Bombay) 1944–45

Bowlers Unchanged Through Both Completed Innings of a Match (Since 1946)
D Shackleton (12–67) and V H D Cannings (8–55): Hampshire v. Kent
(Southampton) 1952
D Shackleton (7–88) and M Heath (13–87): Hampshire v. Derbyshire (Burton
upon Trent) 1958
Rajinder Pal (9–20) and P Sitaram (11–30): Delhi v. Jammu and Kashmir
(Srinagar) 1960–61
B S Crump (12–74) and R R Bailey (8–95): Northamptonshire v. Glamorgan
(Cardiff) 1967

Most Maiden Overs in Succession
6-ball overs: 21 R G Nadkarni – India v. England (Madras) 1963–64
8-ball overs: 16 H J Tayfield – South Africa v. England (Durban) 1956–57

5. Players' Records (All-round Cricket)

Outstanding 'Doubles'
2,000 runs and 200 wickets: G H Hirst (Yorkshire) in 1906
3,000 runs and 100 wickets: J H Parks (Sussex) in 1937
1,000 runs and 200 wickets: A E Trott (Middlesex) in 1899 and 1900
                      A S Kennedy (Hampshire) in 1922
                      M W Tate (Sussex) in 1923, 1924, and 1925

Most 'Doubles'
  16 W Rhodes (Yorkshire)

Fastest 'Double'
  28 June (1906) G H Hirst (Yorkshire) in only sixteen matches

Century and Ten Wickets in an Innings
  V E Walker (108 and 10 for 74): England XI v. Surrey (Oval) 1859
  W G Grace (104 and 10 for 49): MCC v. Oxford U (Oxford) 1886
  F A Tarrant (182* and 10–90): Maharaja of Cooch Behar's XI v. Lord
    Willingdon's XI (Poona) 1918–19

Century and Ten Dismissals in a Match
  R W Marsh (104 and 10 ct): Western Australia v. South Australia (Perth) 1976–77

Double Century and Hat-Trick
  W E Roller (204): Surrey v. Sussex (Oval) 1885

6. Players' Records (Fielding)

Most catches in an Innings
  7 M J Stewart: Surrey v. Northamptonshire (Northampton) 1957
  7 A S Brown: Gloucestershire v. Nottinghamshire (Nottingham) 1966

Most Catches in a Match
  10 W R Hammond: Gloucestershire v. Surrey (Cheltenham) 1928

Most Catches in a Season
  78 W R Hammond (Gloucestershire) 1928

Most Catches in a Career
  1,018 F E Woolley (Kent) 1906–38

7. Players' Records (Wicket-keeping)

Most Dismissals and Catches in an Innings
  8 (8 ct) A T W Grout: Queensland v. Western Australia (Brisbane) 1959–60
  8 (8 ct) D E East: Essex v. Somerset (Taunton) 1985

Most Stumpings in an Innings
  6 H. Yarnold: Worcestershire v. Scotland (Dundee) 1951

Most Dismissals in a Match
  12 (8 ct, 4 st) E Pooley: Surrey v. Sussex (Oval) 1868
  12 (9 ct, 3 st) D Tallon: Queensland v. NSW (Sydney) 1938–39
  12 (9 ct, 3 st) H B Taber: NSW v. South Australia (Adelaide) 1968–69

Most Catches in a Match
  11 A Long: Surrey v. Sussex (Hove) 1964
  11 R W Marsh: Western Australia v. Victoria (Perth) 1975–76
  11 D L Bairstow: Yorkshire v. Derbyshire (Scarborough) 1982

Most Stumpings in a Match
  9 F H Huish: Kent v. Surrey (Oval) 1911

Most Dismissals in a Season
  127 L E G Ames (Kent) – 79 ct, 48 st 1929

Most Catches in a Season
  96 J G Binks (Yorkshire) 1960

Most Stumpings in a Season
  64 L E G Ames (Kent) 1932

Wicket-keepers' 'Double' of 1,000 Runs and 100 Dismissals in a Season
  L E G Ames (Kent) in 1928, 1929, and 1932
  J T Murray (Middlesex) in 1957
Most Dismissals and Catches in a Career
  1,646 (1,471 ct, 175 st) R W Taylor (Derbyshire) 1960–84
Most Stumpings in a Career
  415   L E G Ames (Kent) 1926–51
Largest Innings Without Byes
  672 for 7 d   A P Wickham: Somerset *v.* Hampshire (Taunton) 1899

B. TEST CRICKET ONLY

Key to abbreviations used

E	England	A	Australia
SA	South Africa	WI	West Indies
NZ	New Zealand	I	India
P	Pakistan	SL	Sri Lanka

1. Results Summary

Test Matches – 1876–77 to 1985 inclusive: see opposite page

	Tests	Won	Lost	Drawn	Tied	Toss Won
England	617	227	159	231	–	303
Australia	455	192	134	128	1	228
South Africa	172	38	77	57	–	80
West Indies	241	85	60	95	1	130
New Zealand	170	21	74	75	–	83
India	226	36	82	108	–	113
Pakistan	151	33	38	80	–	80
Sri Lanka	12	–	8	4	–	5

2. Team Records

Highest Innings Total
  903 for 7 d   England *v.* Australia (Oval) 1938
Highest Fourth Innings Totals
  To Win: 406 for 4   India *v.* West Indies (Port-of-Spain) 1975–76
  To Draw: 654 for 5   England *v.* South Africa (Durban) 1938–39
  To Lose: 445   India *v.* Australia (Adelaide) 1977–78
Highest Match Aggregate
  1,981 (for 35 wkts)   South Africa *v.* England (Durban) 1938–39
Lowest Innings Total
  26   New Zealand *v.* England (Auckland) 1954–55
Lowest Match Aggregate (Completed Match)
  234 (for 29 wkts)   Australia *v.* South Africa (Melbourne) 1931–32
Largest Margin of Victory
  Innings and 579 runs: England *v.* Australia (Oval) 1938
The Only Test Tie
  Australia *v.* West Indies (Brisbane) 1960–61
Longest Match
  10 days (43 hours 16 min): South Africa *v.* England (Durban)....................... 1938–39
Side Dismissed Twice in a Day
  India (58 and 82) *v.* England at Manchester on third day 1952

	Tests	Won by								Tied	Drawn
		E	A	SA	WI	NZ	I	P	SL		
England v Australia	257	86	96	–	–	–	–	–	–	–	75
v South Africa	102	46	–	18	–	–	–	–	–	–	38
v West Indies	85	21	–	–	30	–	–	–	–	–	34
v New Zealand	60	30	–	–	–	3	–	–	–	–	27
v India	72	30	–	–	–	–	9	–	–	–	33
v Pakistan	39	13	–	–	–	–	–	3	–	–	23
v Sri Lanka	2	1	–	–	–	–	–	–	–	–	1
Australia v South Africa	53	–	29	11	–	–	–	–	–	–	13
v West Indies	62	–	27	–	19	–	–	–	–	1	15
v New Zealand	15	–	8	–	–	2	–	–	–	–	5
v India	39	–	20	–	–	–	8	–	–	–	11
v Pakistan	28	–	11	–	–	–	–	8	–	–	9
v Sri Lanka	1	–	1	–	–	–	–	–	–	–	–
South Africa v New Zealand	17	–	–	9	–	2	–	–	–	–	6
West Indies v New Zealand	21	–	–	–	7	3	–	–	–	–	11
v India	54	–	–	–	22	–	5	–	–	–	27
v Pakistan	19	–	–	–	7	–	–	4	–	–	8
New Zealand v India	25	–	–	–	–	4	10	–	–	–	11
v Pakistan	27	–	–	–	–	3	–	10	–	–	14
v Sri Lanka	5	–	–	–	–	4	–	–	–	–	1
India v Pakistan	35	–	–	–	–	–	4	6	–	–	25
v Sri Lanka	1	–	–	–	–	–	–	–	–	–	1
Pakistan v Sri Lanka	3	–	–	–	–	–	–	2	–	–	1
	1,022	227	192	38	85	21	36	33	–	1	389

Most Runs in One Day
   One Team: 502 (for 2 wkts)   England v. South Africa (Lord's) 1924
   Both Teams: 588 (for 6 wkts)   England (398 for 6) v India (190 for 0)
   (Manchester) 1936
Least Runs in a Full Day's Play
   95   Australia (80) v. Pakistan (15 for 2) (Karachi) 1956–57
Most Hundreds in an Innings
   5   Australia v. West Indies (Kingston) 1954–55

3. Players' Records (Individual Batting)

Highest Individual Innings
   365★   G St A Sobers: West Indies v. Pakistan (Kingston) 1957–58
Most Runs in a Match
   380   G S Chappell (247★ & 133); Australia v. New Zealand (Wellington) 1973–74
Most Hundreds in Successive Innings
   5   E de C Weekes (West Indies) .... 1947–48 and 1948–49
Most Hundreds in Tests
   30   S M Gavaskar (India): 4 v. E, 5 v. A, 13 v. WI, 2 v. NZ, 5 v. P, 1 v. SL
Most Innings of Fifty and Over
   67   S M Gavaskar (India)
Most Runs in a Series
   974 (Avge 139.14)   D G Bradman: Australia v. England 1930
Most Runs in Tests
   8,654 (Avge 50.60)   S M Gavaskar (India) in 106 Tests
Highest Career Average

	Tests	Inns	NO	Runs	HS	Avge	100s	50s
D G Bradman	52	80	10	6,996	334	99.94	29	13

   Most Runs in a Day
   309   D G Bradman (334): Australia v. England (Leeds) 1930
Most Runs Off One Over
   6-ball: 24   A M E Roberts (462660) off I T Botham WI v. E (Port-of-Spain) 1980–81
      24   S M Patil (4440444) off R G D Willis, I v. E (Manchester) (including a
      no-ball) 1982
   8-ball: 25   B Sutcliffe (66061) and R W Blair (600) off H J Tayfield, NZ v. SA
      (Johannesburg) 1953–54
Fast Scoring
   Fastest 50: 28 min   J T Brown: England v. Australia (Melbourne) 1894–95
   Fastest 100: 70 min   J M Gregory: Australia v. South Africa (Johannesburg) .. 1921–22
   Fastest 100 by number of balls: 56 balls   Viv Richards: West Indies v.
      England (Antigua) 1986
   Fastest 200: 214 min   D G Bradman: Australia v. England (Leeds) 1930
   Fastest 300: 287 min   W R Hammond: England v. New Zealand (Auckland) .. 1932–33
Most Boundaries in an Innings
   57   (5 sixes, 52 fours) J H Edrich (310★): E v. NZ (Leeds) 1965
Most Sixes in an Innings
   10   W R Hammond (336★): E v. NZ (Auckland) 1932–33

4. Players' Records (Batting Partnership)

Record Partnership for Each Wicket
   1st 413   V Mankad and P. Roy: I v. NZ (Madras) 1955–56
   2nd 451   W H Ponsford and D G Bradman: A v. E (Oval) 1934
   3rd 451   Mudassar Nazar and Javed Miandad: P v. I (Hyderabad) 1982–83
   4th 411   P B H May and M C Cowdrey: E v. WI (Birmingham) 1957

216

5th	405	S G Barnes and D G Bradman: A v. E (Sydney)	1946–47
6th	346	J H W Fingleton and D G Bradman: A v. E (Melbourne)	1936–37
7th	347	D St E Atkinson and C C Depeiza: WI v. A (Bridgetown).............	1954–55
8th	246	L E G Ames and G O Allen: E v NZ (Lord's)	1931
9th	190	Asif Iqbal and Intikhab Alam: P v. E (Oval)...........................	1967
10th	151	B F Hastings and R O Collinge: NZ v. P (Auckland)..................	1972–73

5. Players' Records (Bowling)

All Ten Wickets in an Innings
    J C Laker (10 for 53): England v. Australia (Manchester) 1956
Most Wickets in a Match
    19   J C Laker (9 for 37 and 10 for 53): E v. A (Manchester) 1956
Most Wickets in a Series
    49   S F Barnes: England v. South Africa (4 Tests).................................. 1913–14
Most Wickets in Tests
    355 (Avge 23.92) D K Lillee (Australia) in 70 Tests 1971–1984
Hat-tricks (since 1946)

P J Loader	England v. West Indies (Leeds).......................................	1957
L F Kline	Australia v. South Africa (Cape Town)	1957–58
W W Hall	West Indies v. Pakistan (Lahore)	1958–59
G M Griffin	South Africa v. England (Lord's).....................................	1960
L R Gibbs	West Indies v. Australia (Adelaide)	1960–61
P J Petherick	New Zealand v. Pakistan (Lahore) (On debut)......................	1976–77

Wicket with First Ball in Tests (Since 1946)

| R Howorth | England v. South Africa (Oval) .... | 1947 |
| Intikhab Alam | Pakistan v. Australia (Karachi) .... | 1959–60 |

Most Wickets in Debut Match
    16 R A L Massie (8 for 84, 8 for 53) Australia v. England (Lord's)................ 1972
Most Runs Conceded in an Innings
    298 L O Fleetwood-Smith (87–11–298–1): A v. E (Oval) 1938
Most Runs Conceded in a Match
    374 O C Scott (105–2–13–374–9): WI v. E (Kingston)............................ 1929–30
Most Balls Bowled in an Innings
    588 S Ramadhin (98–35–179–2): WI v. E (Birmingham)........................ 1957
Most Balls Bowled in a Match
    774 S Ramadhin (129–51–228–9): WI v. E (Birmingham) 1957

6. Players' Records (All-round Cricket)

Century and Ten Wickets in a Match
    I T Botham (114 and 13 for 106): E v. I (Bombay)..................................... 1979–80
    Imran Khan (117 and 11 for 180): P v. I (Faisalabad)................................. 1982–83
Century and Eight Wickets in an Innings
    I T Botham (108 and 8 for 34): E v. P (Lord's) 1978
Century and Five Wickets on Debut
    B R Taylor (105 and 5 for 86): NZ v. I (Calcutta)..................................... 1964–65
Two Thousand Runs and Two Hundred Wickets in Tests

		Tests	Runs	Wickets
R Benaud	Australia	63	2,201	248
I T Botham	England	79	4,409	343
R J Hadlee	New Zealand	57	2,088	266
Imran Khan	Pakistan	51	2,023	232
Kapil Dev	India	68	2,788	258
G St A Sobers	West Indies	93	8,032	235

7. Players' Records (Fielding)

Most Catches in an Innings
5   V Y Richardson: Australia v. South Africa (Durban) 1935–36
5   Yajurvindra Singh: India v. England (Bangalore) 1976–77
Most Catches in a Match
7   G S Chappell: Australia v. England (Perth) 1974–75
7   Yajurvindra Singh: India v. England (Bangalore) 1976–77
Most Catches in a Series
15   J M Gregory: Australia v. England 1921–21
Most Catches in a Career
122   G S Chappell (Australia) in 87 Tests 1970–84

8. Players' Records (Wicket-keeping)

Most Dismissals in an Innings
7 (all ct)   Wasim Bari: P v. NZ (Auckland) 1978–79
7 (all ct)   R W Taylor: E v. I (Bombay) 1979–80
Most Dismissals in a Match
10 (all ct)   R W Taylor: E v. I (Bombay) 1979–80
Most Dismissals in a Series
28 (all ct)   R W Marsh: A v. E (5 Tests) 1982–83
Most Dismissals and Catches in Tests
355 (343 ct, 12 st)   R W Marsh (Australia) in 96 Tests 1970–84
Most Stumpings in Tests
52   W A S Oldfield (Australia) in 54 Tests
Largest Total Without Byes
659 for 8 d   T G Evans: England v. Australia (Sydney) 1946–47

9. Miscellaneous Records

Most Test Appearances
114   M C Cowdrey (England)
Most Consecutive Test Appearances
90   S M Gavaskar (India) 1971–85
Most Tests as Captain
74   C H Lloyd (West Indies) 1974–85
Youngest Test Player
15 years 124 days   Mushtaq Mohammad: P v. WI (Lahore) 1958–59
Oldest Test Player
52 years 165 days   W Rhodes: E v. WI (Kingston) 1929–30
Most Tests as Umpire
48   F Chester (officiated in England between 1924 and 1955)

C. LIMITED-OVERS CRICKET

1. One-Day International Records 1970–71 to 1985

Highest Total
338 for 5   Pakistan v. Sri Lanka (Swansea) 1983
Lowest Total
45   Canada v. England (Manchester) 1979
Highest Individual Innings
189*   I V A Richards: West Indies v. England (Manchester) 1984
Highest Partnership
224 for 3rd   D M Jones and A R Border: A v. SL (Adelaide) 1984–85

Best Bowling
7 for 51   W W Davis: West Indies v. Australia (Leeds)   1983
Wicket-keeping – Most Dismissals
5 (all ct)   R G de Alwis: Sri Lanka v. Australia (Colombo) 1982–83
5 (all ct)   S M H Kirmani: India v. Zimbabwe (Leicester)   1983
5 (all ct)   R W Marsh: Australia v. England (Leeds)................................   1981
5 (3 ct, 2st)   S Viswanath: India v. England (Sydney).............................. 1984–85
Fielding – Most Catches
4   Salim Malik: Pakistan v. New Zealand (Sialkot) 1984–85
4   S M Gavaskar: India v. Pakistan (Sharjah).. 1984–85

2. NatWest Trophy/Gillette Cup Records – 1963–85

Highest Total
392 for 5   Warwickshire v. Oxfordshire (Birmingham)   1984
Lowest Total
39   Ireland v. Sussex (Hove)   1985
Highest Individual Innings
206   A I Kallicharran: Warwickshire v. Oxfordshire (Birmingham)   1984
Fastest Hundred
77 mins   R E Marshall: Hampshire v. Bedfordshire (Goldington)................   1968
Best Bowling
7 for 15   A L Dixon: Kent v. Surrey (Oval)   1967
Hat-Tricks
J D F Larter   Northamptonshire v. Sussex (Northampton).................   1963
D A D Sydenham   Surrey v. Cheshire (Hoylake)....................................   1964
R N S Hobbs   Essex v. Middlesex (Lord's)   1968
N M McVicker   Warwickshire v. Lincolnshire (Birmingham)   1971
G S Le Roux   Sussex v. Ireland (Hove)   1985
Wicket-keeping – Most Dismissals
6 (5 ct, 1 st)   R W Taylor: Derbyshire v. Essex (Derby)   1981
Fielding – Most Catches
4   A S Brown: Gloucestershire v. Middlesex (Bristol)   1963
4   G Cook: Northamptonshire v. Glamorgan (Northampton)   1972
4   C G Greenidge: Hampshire v. Cheshire (Southampton)   1981
4   D C Jackson: Durham v. Northamptonshire (Darlington)   1984
4   T S Smith: Hertfordshire v. Somerset (St Albans)   1984

3. Benson and Hedges Cup Records – 1972–85

Highest Total
350 for 3   Essex v. Combined Universities (Chelmsford)...........................   1979
Lowest Total
56   Leicestershire v. Minor Counties (Wellington)   1982
Highest Individual Innings
198★   G A Gooch: Essex v. Sussex (Hove)   1982
Fastest Hundred
62 min   M A Nash: Glamorgan v. Hampshire (Swansea)...........................   1976
Best Bowling
7 for 12   W W Daniel: Middlesex v. Minor Counties (East) (Ipswich)   1978
Hat-Tricks
Seven instances: G D McKenzie and K Higgs (Leicestershire), A A Jones
    (Middlesex), M J Procter (Gloucestershire), W Larkins (Northamptonshire),
    E A Moseley (Glamorgan), G C Small (Warwickshire)
Wicket-Keeping – Most Dismissals
5 (all ct)   G Sharp: Northamptonshire v. Middlesex (Lord's)   1974

5 (all ct)   D L Bairstow: Yorkshire *v*. Derbyshire (Bradford) 1975
5 (4 ct, 1 st)   A P E Knott: Kent *v*. Essex (Dartford) 1981
Fielding – Most Catches
5   V J Marks: Combined Universities *v*. Kent (Oxford) 1976

4. John Player League Records – 1969–85

Highest Total
310 for 5   Essex *v*. Glamorgan (Southend) 1983
Lowest Total
23   Middlesex *v*. Yorkshire (Leeds) 1974
Highest Individual Innings
176   G A Gooch: Essex *v*. Glamorgan (Southend) 1983
Fastest Hundred
50 mins   C H Lloyd: Lancashire *v*. Nottinghamshire (Nottingham) 1974
Best Bowling
8 for 26   K D Boyce: Essex *v*. Lancashire (Manchester) 1971
Hat-Tricks
Sixteen instances: A Ward (Derbyshire), R Palmer (Somerset), K D Boyce
    (Essex) G D McKenzie (Leicestershire), R G D Willis and W Blenkiron
    (Warwickshire), A Buss (Sussex), J M Rice (Hampshire), M A Nash
    (Glamorgan) A Hodgson (Northamptonshire), A E Cordle (Glamorgan), C J
    Tunnicliffe (Derbyshire) M D Marshall (Hampshire), I V A Richards
    (Somerset), P W Jarvis (Yorkshire), R M Ellison (Kent).
Wicket-Keeping – Most Dismissals
7 (6 ct, 1 st)   R W Taylor: Derbyshire *v*. Lancashire (Manchester) 1975
Fielding – Most Catches
5   J M Rice: Hampshire *v*. Warwickshire (Southampton) 1978

Appendix 3:
Plans of the Six Test Match Grounds

For anyone going to a Test ground for the first time, or for viewers and listeners to the television and radio commentaries, I thought the following plans to the six grounds would be helpful.

LORD'S, ST JOHN'S WOOD, LONDON
This is the third Lord's ground. The first (1787–1808) was where Dorset Square is now. The second (1809–1813) was at North Bank, Regent's Park; and the third – the present ground – was opened in 1814. It is the home and headquarters of MCC and also houses the TCCB and the NCA.
First Test played: 1884
Number of Tests: 78
Playing area: 5½ acres
Capacity: 26,000

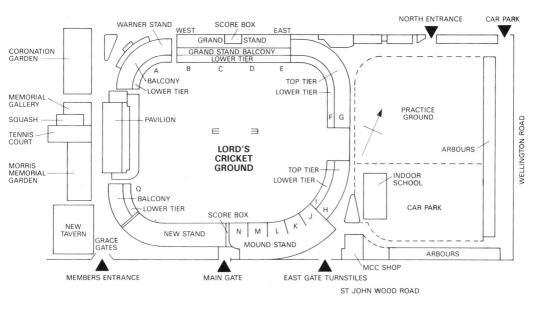

KENNINGTON OVAL, LONDON

Headquarters of Surrey C.C.C. Formerly a market garden, it was opened in 1845.
First Test played: 1880
Number of Tests: 68
Playing area: 7 acres
Capacity: 17,000

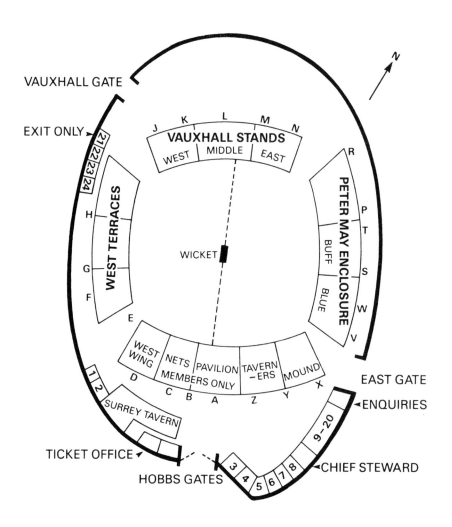

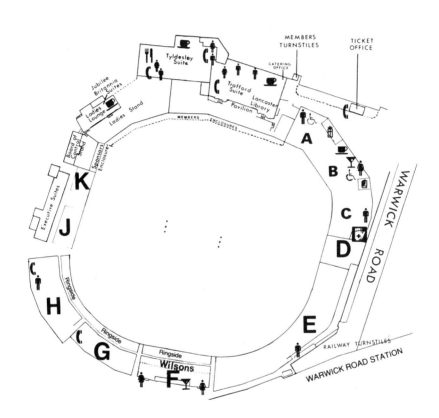

OLD TRAFFORD, MANCHESTER
Headquarters of Lancashire C.C.C. It was opened in 1857.
First Test: 1884
Number of Tests: 54
Playing area: 4½ acres
Capacity: 22,000

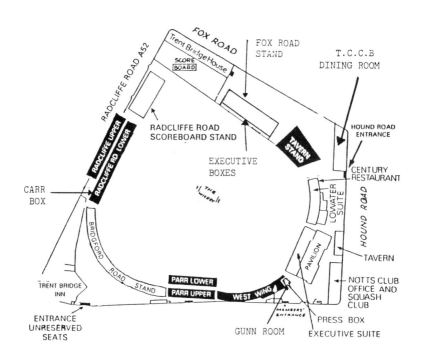

TRENT BRIDGE, NOTTINGHAM

Headquarters of Nottinghamshire C.C.C. It was opened by William Clark in 1838.
First Test: 1899
Number of Tests: 35
Playing area: 6½ acres
Capacity: 15,000

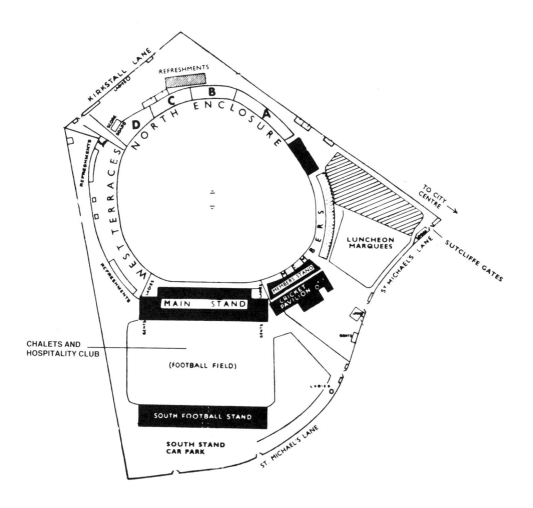

HEADINGLEY, LEEDS
Not officially the headquarters of Yorkshire C.C.C. although the
club does have offices in the pavilion complex. It was opened in
1891.
First Test: 1899
Number of Tests: 48
Playing area: 5 acres
Capacity: 19,000

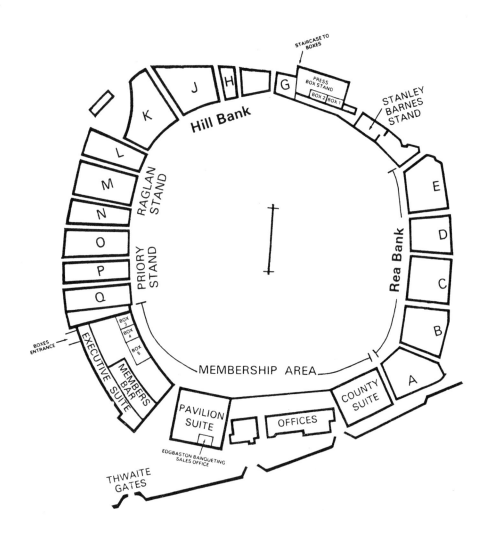

EDGBASTON, BIRMINGHAM
Headquarters of Warwickshire C.C.C. It was opened in 1886.
First Test: 1902
Number of Tests: 23
Playing area: 3¾ acres
Capacity: 18,500

Appendix 4:
Starting a Cricket Library

One of the joys of cricket is its literature. No other game has had such a wealth of books written about it. But quantity is less important than quality, and it is cricket's good fortune that its character has inspired the pens of those who love it. It is also a game which thrives on records, and it has created a new breed of men – the cricket statisticians, who have faithfully recorded all the facts and figures. The result is that few men can claim to have the complete cricket library though my good friend, John Arlott, must come the nearest to it. But don't be disheartened. Even he had to start, so I thought I might try to help any of you who are thinking of doing the same. It is an expensive hobby these days and some of the best books are out of print and difficult to find, in spite of the many excellent booksellers who specialize in cricket books. However, many second-hand booksellers advertise rare cricket books in *The Cricketer*, so it is worth keeping an eye out for them. I have imagined that I am about to start my own library after over sixty years of reading about cricket and so the 14 books described below are essentially a personal choice. They do represent however, a wonderful mixture of history, humour, facts, and figures and all that is best in cricket literature.

The Art of Coarse Cricket by Spike Hughes, Hutchinson, London 1961.
(Describes in a very amusing way a type of cricket played by many of us whose love of the game is greater than our ability to play it).

Barclays's World of Cricket edited by E W Swanton, Collins, 1987.
(A complete encyclopaedia of the game, well arranged, well written and well indexed. Publication coincides with bicentenary of MCC).

The Boundary Book edited by Leslie Frewin, Macdonald & Co Ltd, London 1962.
(Contributions from famous Lord's Taverners).

Cardus on Cricket. Selected by Rupert Hart-Davis, Souvenir Press. (The best example of Neville Cardus's evocative and colourful writings).

Close of Play by A Miller, St Hughes' Press Ltd 1949. (A bedside book guaranteed to bring tears to the eyes).

Cricketer's Companion edited by Alan Ross, Eyre Methuen 1979, Penguin paperback 1981. (A collection of essays, poems, cartoons, and extracts from many of the best books on cricket).

Cricket Prints by R C Robertson – Glasgow, T Werner-Lawrie Ltd 1943. (A fine example of the author's wit and understanding of people).

England Their England by A G Macdonnell, Macmillan, London 1933, Picador Books 1983. (Contains the funniest account of a cricket match ever written).

That Test Match by Sir Home Gordon Duckworth, London 1921. (A somewhat dated book in respect of its sentiments and the style in which it is written. But one can feel the love of the game in almost every line).

Who's Who of Cricketers by Philip Bailey, Philip Thorn, Peter Wynne-Thomas, published by Newnes Books. (A complete who's who of *all* cricketers who have played first class cricket *in England*, with full career records up to the end of the 1983 season. An essential for research – if you can afford it!).

The Wisden Book of Cricket Records 1986.

The Wisden Book of Test Cricket 1877–1984 compiled by Bill Frindall and containing every conceivable type of record.

Wisden Cricketers' Almanack edited by John Woodcock, Queen Anne Press, 123rd edition 1986. (The Bible of Cricket and the *first* book for any library).

The Young Cricketers' Tutor by J Nyren Gay and Bird, Sportsman's Classic Series 1902. (The story of the famous Hampshire Club – Hambledon).

Appendix 5:
Answers to the Quiz

1. Sixteen.

2. No, not in the first instance. But if the umpires decide that the light is too bad to continue, they must then ask the batsmen at the crease whether they wish to go off, or to continue play. If they decide to continue and the light later deteriorates still further, the batsmen may *then* appeal to the umpires.

3. A minimum of 20 overs must be bowled, provided there is no interval nor interruption of play.

4. Four.

5. The team with the most wins will be the winner.

6. When the bowler starts his run-up or bowling action.

7. Four ways: Run out; Handling the Ball; Obstructing the Field; Hitting the Ball Twice.

8. Out. Hit wicket.

9. Thirty-eight inches in length; 4¼ inches wide.

10. Stumped, hit wicket, run out, handled the ball, obstructing the field.

11. At the fall of a wicket.

12. In a two innings match the side which bats first and leads *by 200 runs* in a match of five days or more, *by 150 runs* in a three-day or four-day match, *by 100* runs in a two-day match, or *by 75 runs* in a one-day match, has the option of asking the other side to follow-on.

13. If a batsman is out first ball for 0 in each innings he is said to have made a 'King Pair'.

14. Eighty-five.

15. Not later than 15 minutes before the time scheduled for the match to start, or before the time agreed upon for play to start.

16. Five feet in width on either side of a line joining the centre of the middle of the stumps.

17. No, although he may object to the substitute acting as wicket-keeper.

18. Yes, but only if the ball has first touched the bat or person of the batsman.

19. Yes. The bowler's back foot must land 'within and not touching the return crease'.

20. When he wilfully strikes the ball a second time with his bat or person *with the sole purpose of guarding his wicket*.

21. Yes. From an overthrow (he might be out of his crease) or from a penalty when the ball he has struck a second time is stopped by something other than by a fielder – e.g. if it hits a helmet or the fielder stops the ball with his cap. Penalty 5 runs to the batsman.

22. Allow a fresh bowler to bowl at that end.

23. If in the opinion of the umpire it constitutes an attempt to intimidate the batsman.

24. No. The ball becomes dead. Nor is the batsman out if the ball lodges in a fielder's helmet.

25. No.

26. Anyone. But they must *not* waste time in doing so.

27. Yes, at any time of a match, irrespective of its duration.

28. Yes, providing he is definitely setting off for his first run.

29. No. It is only a catch 'off the hand *holding the bat*'.

30. Two.

31. An off-break bowled by a *left* arm bowler.

32. Twenty-eight inches above the ground.

33. No. A fielder must be within the playing area throughout the act of making the catch. Six runs would be scored.

34. Call 'dead ball', but allow the run already scored.

35. On an appeal of How's that? Or probably: How's that out handled the ball? the umpire would *have* to give the batsman out. The batsman must never handle the ball whilst it is in play *without the consent of the fielding side*.

36. The incoming batsman is timed out if he *wilfully* takes more than two minutes to come in – the two minutes being taken from the moment a wicket falls until the new batsman steps on to the field of play. But the umpire must decide that the delay was *wilful* and not due to some accident or unforeseen circumstance.

37. Yes, if he has made no attempt to play a stroke. But if he *has* tried to play the ball, then he is *not* out.

38. If the ball, not having been called 'wide' or 'no ball' is *unintentionally* deflected by the batsman's dress or person – except for a hand holding the bat – the umpire will signal leg-bye. But he will only do so if the batsman has attempted to play the ball with his bat, or has tried to avoid being hit by the ball. But if no attempt at playing a stroke has been made, then the umpire does NOT call leg-bye.

39. Four wides – *not* four byes.

40. No. It is the batsman who has hit the ball who is out caught. The non-striker is *not* run out.

Index

Index

Adcock, N A T 105, 122
Advisory County Cricket
    Committee 26
Alderman, T M 76
Alexander, F C M 53
Allen, D A 61–2
Archer, R G 56
Armstrong, W W 21
Art of Coarse Cricket, The 227
Ashes, the 20, 23–4, 46–50, 57,
    69–75
    winners and holders 48

Bailey, T E 56, 63, 211
Bannerman, C 20
Bardsley, W 21
Barlow, E J 111
Barnes, S F 21, 217
Barrington, K F 59, 61, 64,
    106, 179
Bedser, A V 24, 56, 88, 94, 124
Beldham, Billy 12
Benaud, R 52, 53, 55, 98, 100,
    101, 217
Benson and Hedges Cup 24, 29,
    37
    previous winners 37
Blackham, J M 20
Bligh, the Hon. Ivo 48
Board of Control 21, 26
Bonnor, G J 20
Border, A R 142, 218
Botham, I T 24, 76, 77, 134–5,
    146, 166, 211, 217
Boundary Book, The 227
Boycott, G 24, 63, 64, 69, 112,
    118, 130, 132
Bradman, Sir Don 23, 24, 84,
    128, 130, 132, 150, 210,
    211, 216

Brearley, J M 49, 76, 77, 78
Brett, Thomas 11
Bright, R J 77
Britannic Assurance County
    Championship *see* Cricket,
    County Championship
Brown, D J 66, 68
Butcher, B F 59

Camacho, G S 64
Cardus on Cricket 228
Chapman, A P F 50
Chappell, G S 24, 71, 73, 74,
    118, 121, 128, 216, 218
Chappell, I M 66, 69, 71, 74, 121
Chappell, Trevor 121
Clark, William 14, 16
Close, D B 59, 61, 180–1
Collins, A E J 21
Compton, D C S 24, 46, 55–7
    passim, 82, 210
Connolly, A N 68
Cornhill Tests, 25, 29
County Championship *see*
    Cricket, County
    Championship
Cowdrey, M C 24, 59–67
    passim, 112, 118, 216, 218
Cricket
    clubs
        Hambledon 11, 12
        Marylebone (MCC) 13, 26,
        27
        Melbourne 16
        South Wales 18
        White Conduit 12, 13, 26
    Council 25
    County 14
        Championship 20, 25, 26,
        29, 32–3

Cricket—*contd*.
  history
    early 10–21
    1920–38 21–3
    post-war 24–5
  laws 20, 27, 169–72
  League 42
  limited over 24, 44–5
  techniques
    batting 148–68
    bowling 159–62
    fielding 163–6
    wicket-keeping 166–8
  Test 17, 18, 20–31 *passim*,
    51–79
    laws 29–31
  village 25, 29, 43–4
Cricket Prints 228
Cricketer Cup (and Moët &
  Chandon Award) for Old
  Boys' Teams 25, 43
Cricketer's Companion 228
Cromwell, Oliver 10
Currie Cup 17
Currie, Sir Donald 17

Darling, J 21
Davidson, A K 52, 57, 96, 101,
  122
Dell, A R 71, 74
Denness, M H 122
Derwick, John 10
Dexter, E R 24, 58–9
Dilley, G R 76, 77
d'Oliveira, B L 64–74 *passim*,
  121

Eastwood, K H 71, 74
Edrich, J H 59, 64, 66, 71, 73
Edrich, W J 24, 55, 56
Edward I, King 10
Elliott, C 68
England Their England 228
Evans, T G 24, 94, 124–5, 136,
  218

Farnes, K 122
Faulkner, G A 21
Favell, L 52
Felix, N 14
Fletcher, K W R 46, 71, 73, 74–5

Foster, R E 21
Fry, C B 21, 210

Gatting, M W 146
Gavaskar, S 24, 118, 132, 216,
  218, 219
Gibbs, L R 24, 64, 65, 217
Giffen, G 20
Gillette Cup 24, 34
Gleeson, J W 68
Gover, A R 177
Gower, D 50, 134, 142, 166
Grace, W G 18–20, 108, 177–8,
  180, 210, 213
Graveney, T W 64, 112, 211
Gregory, D W 20
Gregory, J M 21, 105, 122, 216,
  218
Gregory, S E 21
Griffith, C 59, 61, 105
Grimmett, C 23
Grout, A T W 53, 96, 213
Gunn, G 21

Hadlee, R J 24, 144, 159, 217
Hadlee, W A 144
Hall, W W 52, 53, 59, 61, 62,
  64, 105, 122, 217
Hambledon *see* Cricket, Clubs
Hammond, W R 23, 81, 118,
  126, 210, 213, 216
Hampshire, J H 71, 73
Hanif Mohammad 24, 210, 211
Harris, David 12
Hassett, A L 55, 56
Harvey, R N 24, 52, 100
Hendren, E H 181
Hill, C 21
Heine, P 105, 122
Hirst, G H 21, 213
Hobbs, J B 21–4 *passim*, 210
Holding, M 24, 122, 159
Hollies, W E 84
Hunte, C C 53, 58
Hutton, Sir Len 24, 50, 56, 91,
  180, 210

Illingworth, Ray 46, 66, 70–5
  passim, 136
Imperial Cricket Conference
  20–4 *passim*, 51

Imran Khan 24, 217
International Cricket
    Conference 24, 29
Inverarity, R J 66–8

Jackson, Hon. F S 21
Jardine, D R 18
Jarman, B N 66, 67
Jenner, T J 46, 71, 73, 74
Jessop, G L 21
John Player League 24, 29,
    37–40
  previous winners 40
Johnston, W A 56
Jones, I J 64–5

Kanhai, R 53, 63
Kapil Dev 24, 217
King, L A 64
Kline, L F 53, 63, 217
Knott, A P E 64, 65, 71, 73, 74,
    94, 124–5, 136, 166, 220

Laker, J C 24, 56, 92, 212, 217
Larwood, H 21, 23, 105, 122,
    176
Lawry, W M 66, 69, 74
Leer, George 11
Lever, P 71, 73, 74
Lillee, D K 24, 69, 71–5 *passim*,
    122, 134, 217
Lillywhite, James 17, 20
Lindwall, R R 56, 85, 91, 105,
    116, 122
Lloyd, C H 24, 64, 128, 138,
    218, 220
Lock, G A R 56, 63–4, 92
Lockwood, W H 21
Lohmann, G A 21
Lord, Thomas 12, 13
Lord's 13, 14, 25, 221
Luckhurst, B W 69, 73

Macartney, C G 21, 210
McDonald, E A 21, 52, 105
Mackay, K 52, 63
McKenzie, G D 68, 69, 96, 122,
    219, 220
Maclaren, A C 20
Mailey, A A 21, 212
Mallett, A A 68

Mann, Noah 11–12
Marsh, R W 71, 74, 77, 94, 213,
    218, 219
May, P B H 24, 55, 56, 93, 216
MCC *see* Cricket, Clubs,
    Marylebone
Meckiff, I W 53, 54
Melbourne Cricket Club *see*
    Cricket, Clubs, Melbourne
Miller, K R 85, 87, 91, 102,
    105, 122
Minor County Championship
    (United Friendly
    Insurance) 20, 27, 40–2
  previous champions 41–2
Moët & Chandon Award *see*
    Cricketer Cup
Morris, A R 46, 56–7, 86
Murdoch, W L 20
Murray, D L 61
Mynn, Alfred 14

National Cricket Association
    (NCA) 27
National Village Championship,
    (Norsk Hydro Fertilizers)
    see Cricket, Village
NatWest Trophy 29, 34–6
  previous winners 36
Newman, J 178–9
Noble, M A 21
Norsk Hydro Fertilizers Cup *see*
    Cricket, Village
Nourse, A D Senior 21
Nurse, S M 64
Nyren, John 11

O'Keefe, K J 71, 74
Old, C M 76, 77
O'Neill, N 52
O'Reilly, W 23

Packer, K 116, 121, 125, 136,
    141
Parks, J M 59, 61
Parr, George 14, 16, 17
Peel, R 20
Pilch, Fuller 14
Plunket, Lord 17
Plunket Shield 17

Pocock, P I 63, 64, 212
Pollock, R G 24, 126
Price, W F F 178
Procter, M J 116, 210, 219
Prudential World Cup *see*
    World Cup

Ramadin, S 52, 212, 217
Randall, Derek 49
Ranji Trophy 18
Ranjitsinji, K S (Ranji) 20–1
Redpath, R 66, 71, 74, 121
Reeves, W 177, 180
Rhodes, W 21, 212, 213, 218
Richards, B A 24, 114, 128
Richards, I V A (Viv) 24, 128,
    166, 218, 220
Richardson, T 21
Roberts, A M E 122
Robins, R W V 180
Rowan, L 72, 74

Schwarz, R O 21
Shackleton, D 58–9, 61–2, 212
Sheahan, A P 66
Sheffield, Earl of 17
Sheffield Shield 17
Shell Tournament 17
Sheppard, Rev. David 176–7,
    179
Sherwell, P W 21
Shrewsbury, A 20
Simpson, R B 52
Simpson, R T 55, 118
Small, John 11, 12
Smith, Alan 106
Smith, C A 17
Snow, J A 63–6 *passim*, 71–5
    passim
Sobers, G S 24, 52, 53, 58, 59,
    63–5 *passim*, 91, 97, 108,
    118, 128, 134, 210, 216, 217
Solomon, J S 52, 53, 58, 210
Spofforth, F R 20
Sporting Times 47
Sports Council 26
Stackpole, K R 71, 74
Statham, J B 104, 105, 122
Stevens, 'Lumpy' 12
Stewart, M J 59, 213
Stoddart, A E 20

Stollmeyer, J B 102
Sueter, Tom 11
Sutcliffe, B 24, 216
Sutcliffe, H 21

Tate, M W 21, 81, 88, 213
Tennyson, Lord 178–9
Taylor, H W 21
Taylor, R W 136, 166, 214, 218,
    220
Test and County Cricket Board
    (TCCB) 27, 51
Test Matches 51–79 *see also*
    Cornhill Tests
Texaco Trophy *see* World Cup
That Test Match 228
Thomson, J R 122, 185
Titmus, F J 59, 61
Trueman, F S 24, 59–61 *passim*,
    102, 104–5, 116, 122, 180
Trumper, V T 21, 211
Turner, C T B 20
Turner, Mike 146
Tyldesley, J T 21
Tyson, F H 104, 112, 122, 178

Underwood, D L 46, 66, 68, 71,
    74, 141
United Friendly Insurance
    Minor County
    Championship *see* Minor
    County Championship

Vernon, G F 18
Voce, W 105

Walcott, C L 24, 89
Walters, K D 66, 71, 74
Ward, William 14
Ward, Ted 67, 68
Warner, P 21
Watson, W 55, 63
Weekes, E D 24, 90, 216
Who's Who of Cricketers 228
Willis, R G D 24, 72–8 *passim*,
    166, 220
William Younger Club Cricket
    Championship Cup 25, 42,
    43
Wisden, John 14

Wisden Book of Cricket Records
228
Wisden Book of Test Cricket 228
Wisden Cricketer's Almanack 14,
18, 51
Woolley, F E 21, 126, 146,
213
World of Cricket, Barclays 227

World Cup, Texaco (former
sponsor – Prudential
Assurance Company) 25,
29, 44
Worrell, Sir Frank 24, 58–62
passim, 97, 138

Young Cricketer's Tutor 11, 228